the way not only to freedom from ego-personality but also to the blossoming of that personality into a vessel for wisdom and compassion.

—**SIMEON B. MIHAYLOV,**
  creator of the *Seeker to Seeker* Substack

Living Awakeness is a rare and compelling integration of deep realization and practical guidance, bridging the strengths of both Theravada and Zen traditions with remarkable clarity. Stephen Mugen Snyder, Roshi, offers a precise and experience-based map of Awakening that doesn't stop at insight but shows how to embody it through the lived qualities of Awakeness. This is a valuable and trustworthy guide for serious practitioners seeking not just Awakening but a life aligned with it.

—**MARK COLEMAN,**
  Dharma teacher and author

Mugen Roshi's latest work fills a gap in the literature on Awakening. In an organized, intimate, and comprehensive way, he brings to life the specific qualities, attributes, and factors that are developed in spiritual practice. By elucidating the subtler dimensions cultivated in sincere practice, this book should provide strong guidance and deep encouragement, especially for those experiencing the common pitfall of reaching a plateau. I especially appreciated Mugen's inclusion of emotionally rich qualities, such as delight, tenderness, and gratitude, to go along with more commonly discussed ones, such as unification, surrender, and service. A wonderful guide to the scenic route that is the spiritual path.

—**PAUL GYODO AGOSTINELLI, SENSEI**
  founder of the Eon Zen Center

Living Awakeness explores what is revealed in Awakeness and the practices that bring it to life. It is an intimate work, inviting readers into the inner life of spiritual awakening. Like its author, this book is something to treasure.

—**MARK SHOPE,**

> associate professor of law, National Yang Ming Chiao Tung University School of Law (Taiwan); founder of the Asia Network for Contemplative Legal and Policy Studies

As a devoted student of Mugen Roshi's, I found that *Living Awakeness* mirrors Roshi's direct in-person teachings, which I have absorbed and found transformative. Offering depth, authenticity, and clarity, the book is enhanced by Roshi's highly effective communication style. *Living Awakeness* clearly lays out a path and guides readers through meditations and evaluations that support these timeless Theravada and Zen practices, engaging modern-day practitioners with trust and confidence on the path to Awakening.

—**CORY DAISETSU SCHREIBER,**

> author of *Wildwood: Cooking from the Source in the Pacific Northwest, Rustic Fruit Desserts,* and *Zen Kitchen Mind: A Chef's Journey Through Cause and Effect* (Fall 2026)

Mugen's excellent work builds bridges in many directions. With a background in both Zen and Theravada Buddhist practice, he helpfully discusses Awakening from both perspectives. And while this book includes a tremendous amount of information that Mugen has accumulated over many years, and is extremely helpful in explaining millennia of doctrine, it is firmly rooted in and aimed directly toward the reader's personal practice. Indeed, Zen practice is always fundamentally experiential, and this book helps provide guideposts both to those setting out on the path as well as to those well along the journey. Mugen tackles complex topics with great clarity. For the armchair Buddhist, this is an invitation to deepen practice; for the experienced practitioner, it offers a framework of reference. An invaluable contribution.

—DHARMA-JOY REICHERT,
    abbot and head priest of the Zen Center of Los Angeles

LIVING AWAKENESS

LIVING AWAKENESS

Embodying Your Awakening

STEPHEN MUGEN SNYDER, ROSHI

Buddha's
Heart Press

Buddha's Heart Press
awakeningdharma.org
Midland, MI, USA

Library of Congress Control Number: 2026903226

ISBN: 979-8-9881720-4-8 (paperback)
ISBN: 979-8-9881720-5-5 (e-book)

Editing and proofreading by Lynn Slobogian
Copyediting by Eva van Emden
Cover design by Jazmin Welch (fleck creative studio)
Interior design by Alex Hennig (ClearDesign)
Cover artwork: "Tessvänri maastik" by Lilly Walther, 1899, Tartu Art Museum, Estonia. Via Unsplash.
E-book created by LitBridge

CONTENTS

FOREWORD

*Whether we experience the surrender of self
for a moment or a lifetime, our lives . . . are . . .
deeply enriched.*

STEPHEN MUGEN SNYDER, ROSHI, experienced spiritual insight at a very young age. Through a lifetime of intensive study and training, he achieved mastery in both the Theravada and Zen schools of Buddhism. His many books, as well as in-person and online teachings, provide support for spiritual practitioners around the world. With this book, *Living Awakeness*, Stephen offers his teaching on what Awakening is, and he provides new practices to resolve psychological obstacles that can act as a barrier to experiencing, integrating, and embodying profound spiritual experiences.

In his prior book *Liberating the Self*, Stephen identified the difficulty for students who have deep experiences but fail to integrate them into daily life because of deeply seated psychological habits and triggers. To counter this problem, Stephen introduced ways to mature the personality. Still, many students required further teaching. As Stephen writes, "I began tracking this in my practice while working with hundreds of students, noting the qualities of Awakeness I saw in them. . . . Through studying my students, I identified the qualities of Awakeness included in this book."

Based on Stephen's in-depth study and teaching, *Living Awakeness* provides powerful practical guidance to students who have had confirmed Awakening experiences, helping them identify, practice, develop, and integrate the qualities of Awakening. These qualities arise spontaneously when we let go of the idea that we're a self—separate from others, from the living world, from the great universe itself. Whether we experience the surrender of self for a moment or a lifetime, our lives and the lives of countless others are liberated and deeply enriched. This book is a doorway into just that kind of embodied experience. Please don't miss it.

Mark Sando Mininberg, Roshi

PREFACE

By engaging with the practices in this book, students will more fully integrate and function from the transcendent experiences of Awakeness.

I FIRST ENCOUNTERED Buddhism when I was three years old. My family was traveling in Japan and stopped for a few nights in Tokyo. One blustery fall afternoon, we went for a walk through the city. As the wind gusted into stillness, I happened to see a man running down the sidewalk. He had a shaved head, which was extraordinarily rare in those days, and black robes billowed behind him.

When my eyes locked on him, I felt an instant connection, a unity of identity, and a sense of being gobsmacked by reality. There I was! Somehow, I was seeing an externalized version of me. I was that monk, and he was me. We were always connected, intertwined even, in an undivided unity. This was my first experience of knowing wholeness.

Starting in my late teens, I began delving into Buddhism, vividly recalling the Oneness with the Zen monk in Tokyo many years earlier. During this time, I found a deep unbroken grounding in meditation and in Buddhism generally. Over the next fifty years, my spiritual path led to my own Awakening and eventual development as a Buddhist teacher and mentor.

My role as a teacher began quite unexpectedly twenty years ago. I attended a two-month Theravada *samatha* retreat with the Venerable Pa Auk Sayadaw, a renowned Buddhist teacher and celebrated meditation master. Following the completion of the Theravada traditional *samatha* (purification of mind) meditations and practices, he authorized me to teach these ancient practices and meditations. This was both an unprecedented honor and a grave responsibility; I would be mentoring students on the 2,500-year-old path of purification and Awakening.

During the COVID-19 pandemic lockdown, I began working actively with two roshis. I completed formal *kōan* study (about 600 *kōans*) and then was invited to the mind-to-mind dharma transmission process with my teacher Mark Sando Mininberg, Roshi. In 2025, my teacher completed the final seal of the mind-to-mind transmission, called Inka Shomei. These processes left me eager to offer these ancient Zen/Chan practices and teachings to modern students. I now also teach the formal Zen *kōan* practice and the deep Absolute meditation called *shikantaza*.

Why do I teach both Theravada and Zen practices? The traditional Theravada practices and meditations support a gradual ripening of consciousness and a releasing of what is conceptual, conditioned reality in favor of what is without condition—the Absolute. The culminating Awakening experience of Theravada Buddhism is Cessation, also called *Nibbāna*. In contrast, the Zen practices focus on supporting a sudden, direct Awakening called *kenshō*. By combining these practices, I can support students in improving their emotional intelligence, deepening their contact with the Absolute, and developing greater psychological maturity.

Why focus on Awakeness? As I witnessed and confirmed a growing number of student Awakenings, both *kenshō* and Cessation, I saw that many students struggle to integrate and embody these profound experiences. Neither Buddhist tradition had much to support the integration of their realizations.

So I began working with students' psychological habits of personality. By this I mean working with their reactivity when faced with personality triggers. The students were having Awakening experiences but were unable to live from that experience because of habitual behaviors and patterns of personality. This undigested, unresolved personality material is addressed in my book *Liberating the Self*.

But even though I had introduced ways to mature the personality to carry the impact of Awakening more gracefully, I saw that there needed to be further clarification and development of the actual qualities of Awakeness. I began tracking this in my practice while working with hundreds of students, noting the qualities of Awakeness I saw in them. To be clear, not all students are refined in every Awakeness quality. Most students have a few Awakeness qualities that are more natural and accessible; the other qualities are out of reach or harder to perceive because of various habits of mind and personality patterns.

Through studying my students, I identified the qualities of Awakeness included in this book. I link these qualities with the various practices I teach to help us further embody our Awakeness. By doing so, *Living Awakeness* allows us to develop those qualities that are less apparent, while also providing our teacher-student relationships with identifiable goals and areas of development. By engaging with the practices in this book, students will more fully integrate and function from the transcendent experiences of Awakeness.

INTRODUCTION

> *Part of the Awakening realization is knowing that every sentient being is awake right now. . . . Consider clouds shielding the sun from view: If we live in persistent cloudy weather patterns, we may conclude clouds are all that is ever present. Only when we directly experience beaming, brilliant, penetrating sunlight do we recognize the ever-present sun.*

IN THE ZEN TRADITION, an important lineage document is the *Denkoroku* (*Record of the Transmission of the Light*). The *Denkoroku* conveys the deep Awakening story of all living Buddhas, from Shakyamuni Buddha to Japanese Zen teachers in the 1200s. The echo of the Buddha's deep realization of ultimate truth, of ultimate reality, called the Absolute, invites and guides students of Awakening today.

In *Living Buddha Zen*, lineage teacher Lex Hixon shares his version of the *Denkoroku*, relaying Shakyamuni Buddha's deep Awakening story: "From beneath the bodhi tree before dawn, Shakyamuni perceives the morning star directly and awakens beyond all Awakening, exclaiming: 'I, the broad earth, and all conscious beings are enlightened and effortlessly manifest the Great Way together.'" The Buddha does not exclaim "will one day be enlightened." He says, "I, the broad earth, and all conscious beings ARE enlightened." He uses the present tense in this potent statement, telling us that each conscious being is enlightened right in this moment.

Part of the Awakening realization is knowing that every sentient being is awake right now and has always been awake, even if they do not perceive it experientially. Consider clouds shielding the sun from view: If we live in persistent cloudy weather patterns, we may conclude clouds are all that is ever present. Only when we directly experience beaming, brilliant, penetrating sunlight do we recognize the ever-present sun.

The Buddha is also communicating that he is no longer simply an individual identity. He is present in recognizable physical form, but he no longer abides as or in his personal self-identity—his prior sense of self-images and self-identities, his history, his memories, his body, his emotions, or his behaviors—as ultimate truth. He now recognizes his self-identity as deep unmanifest Absence; profound peace;

profound stillness; all-encompassing, unrestricted love; innate goodness; and radiant Presence from the ninth *Jhāna*, the Absolute realm. He is actively and fully experiencing and effortlessly aligned with the Absolute—"the Great Way," the unconditioned source of all creation and manifestation—in human form. The Absolute is experiencing him as its expression and manifestation of Awakeness.

My focus as a Sōtō Zen, Rinzai Zen, and Theravada Buddhist teacher is, simply put, Awakening. Through the deep Theravada Awakening experiences of Cessation (*nirodha samapati*) and the direct Zen Awakening experiences of *kenshō*, my teaching emphasizes deep nonconceptual meditation while opening to the Absolute. Students practicing Theravada develop the deep concentration level of absorption or *jhāna*. Those practicing Zen develop silent illumination meditation, or *shikantaza*, as well as the profoundly revealing practice of formal *kōan* practice (nonconceptual spiritual exchanges between Zen master and student).

By cultivating these practices, a student can pass through the layers of cultural and personal beliefs telling them that the conditioned, relative world and the sense of "me" are primary reality. When this core belief is shattered, even temporarily, the student can directly experience Awakening like the Buddha described, and the effects are life-altering.

After this experience, we can never again fully believe "I am exclusively this personality and body." We have seen behind the curtain of our self, our family, and our culture.

We are temporarily liberated, free from the bindings and restraints of everyday reality. Within each of us—in fact, within all living beings—is the potential to be deeply awake when our self-identity is vanquished like this. In the Zen tradition, we call this potency Buddha nature: our potential to be fully realized, deeply awake Buddhas.

In this book I focus primarily on "Awakeness," the alive, refreshed, enduring state of consciousness and awareness following a heart-opening, *jhāna*, *kenshō*, or deep Cessation experience. This quality of Awakeness is one of the hallmarks I watch for when assessing students' realization or Awakening experiences.

Awakeness can be easily understood if we consider normal awareness and consciousness as being like a small home satellite dish. Following an Awakening experience, the dish expands. Our perception, awareness, and consciousness begin tracking a broader, deeper, more refined Absolute reality. This amplification is our newfound Awakeness.

In this state, we naturally begin to experience the Absolute as a kind of flow, a current of Awakeness. Part of our journey home is to develop the ability, interest, and techniques to align with this current, and investigating our behavior to conform to the Absolute becomes a critical ongoing practice. It takes time. Using a spiritual journal and doing regular one-on-one work with an experienced teacher are also needed to fully embody and express this ongoing, expanding Awakeness, to potentially realize our Buddha nature.

My lineage is teaching the *jhānas*, the traditional *samatha* practices and meditations, the heart practices called the *brahmavihāras*, *kōans*, *shikantaza*, and Cessation. These are all needed for the journey of deep Awakening and the subsequent critical integration and embodiment of Awakeness. If we cannot live from realization, it does not have much benefit.

In this book I focus primarily on meditations and practices with particular exercises to acquaint or reacquaint with Buddha nature and to support Awakeness potentially flowering to Buddhahood.

PART I

The Qualities of Awakeness

When we orient our actions and behavior toward the benefit of all sentient beings, we loosen our historical grip on our increasingly desperate personality aches.

MY PRACTICE AS A TEACHER for the past twenty years is to track student experiences and the impacts of Awakening. In the process of confirming the depth and breadth of a student's Awakening, I use the qualities of Awakeness to help gauge the depth and breadth of an Awakening experience.

Some students will have minor, shallower Awakening experiences, where only a few qualities of Awakening are present. I encourage the deepening of contact with and experience of these qualities. These shallower Awakenings are deeply impactful on the student's identity and consciousness, yet insufficient to qualify as a stream entry. (Stream entry is the first level of Awakening in both the Zen and Theravada traditions.)

In all the students whose Awakenings I confirmed were deep enough to cross the threshold of stream entry, all of the following qualities were present and functioning. These twelve qualities of Awakeness originate in the Absolute. Each is without personality or identity in the customary sense. We engage and cultivate our contact with these qualities of Awakeness as they spontaneously arise in awareness:

1	Wholesomeness	7	Tenderness
2	Gratitude	8	Flow
3	Delight	9	Purity
4	Unification	10	Aloneness
5	Beingness	11	Surrender
6	Nonconceptual perception	12	Service

I will discuss each quality and offer an exercise for us to more deeply penetrate, explore, and understand our relationship and history with these Awakening qualities.

WHOLESOMENESS

TO UNDERSTAND WHAT wholesomeness is, we should first explore unwholesomeness. Generally speaking, unwholesomeness is rooted in selfishness and personal greed. In the Zen precept "Cease from evil," I define evil as being focused nearly exclusively on an individual personality's desires. It is when we persist in trying to get what we want regardless of the cost or impact on others. We often blind ourselves to the risk of harming others by our selfishness.

When we turn toward unwholesomeness, we are often motivated by the fear of loss or failure. We may feel so desperate internally that we grasp frantically for a resolution to save us from certain peril, if not outright extinction.

The opposite of this plane of selfishness and fear is wholesomeness. Typically, wholesomeness has a feeling or tone of tolerant expansiveness or unrestricted openness. Wholesomeness by its nature and definition cultivates what is whole, complete, and united—an experiential Oneness. The pure precept "Do only good" is wholesomeness in intention, function, and behavior. When we orient our actions and behavior toward the benefit of all sentient beings, we loosen our historical grip on our increasingly desperate personality aches.

We can recognize wholesomeness by its uplifting, impersonal movement and its virtuous intention. Wholesomeness orients toward the warmhearted unifying aspects of any situation and repeatedly shifts away from divisive motivations. Our alignment is with the empirically good, the complete thoroughgoing truth, and the nondual, undivided function of the Absolute.

When I was first engaging with wholesomeness, I found it challenging. I could contact wholesomeness for others quite easily, but revealing wholesomeness in myself was difficult. It was my firm belief in my own unworthiness that was my resistance. I had to painstakingly examine each deeply held negative self-belief to reveal its truth or falsity. As you may expect, I found most of the closely held beliefs about my unworthiness to be unsustainable when examined through the lens of truth. My practice rule was: If it is true, I hold it dear. If false, it must be discarded.

Wholesomeness Exercise

What is your understanding of your wholesomeness?

When are you naturally in contact with wholesomeness?

What prevents you from opening to your wholesomeness?

What would life look like if you opened more fully to wholesomeness?

GRATITUDE

GRATITUDE'S COUNTERPOINT IS thanklessness and entitlement. Brain researchers suggest that humans have a greater inclination to store and recall with vivid attention the negative life experiences over the positive ones. This is a kind of protection, a defense.

Thanklessness generally has the attitude of routine expectation. The person expects whatever is occurring and is slightly disinterested.

Resistance to gratitude can occur because we feel that our desired object is in limited supply. We feel we have to claw out, and desperately cling to, what we need. Thus, we may hold mixed feelings about having desires and about the outcomes of either succeeding or failing to secure the desired object.

It's vitally important to not only recognize but to carefully cultivate and accumulate what is most beneficial in life. We need to practice gratitude, raising our appreciation for what is uplifting and enriching. By identifying and gathering our positive life experiences, we orient toward what is wholesome, thoroughly unified, in a nondual field of unsurpassed love and complete acceptance. When we practice gratitude, we connect more to the buoyancy, the uplift, of the love, Presence, and acceptance of the Absolute.

My initial resistance to gratitude was because I felt my success in securing desired objects was solely linked to my personal efforts. In other words, I held the conviction that I had not received anything that I did not bring about through some self-motivated action.

I began working with gratitude by finding one aspect of my life for which I easily felt gratitude. It was something small and simple. Once I could contact even a small amount of gratitude, I could begin expanding it into other aspects of my life.

Gratitude Exercise

What is your understanding of your gratitude?

When are you naturally grateful?

What prevents you from opening to your gratitude?

What would life look like if you opened more fully
to gratitude?

List three things you are grateful for in your life
today.

DELIGHT

WHEN FIRST ENCOUNTERING objective, universal delight, we can meet resistances. One way that delight can be blocked is by our perception of unworthiness in a multitude of forms. Our self-perception of deficit, our strong belief that we are irredeemably broken, can make us feel that we are not worthy of beneficial experiences. When good things happen, we expect they will be taken away, or our belief in our unworthiness causes the delight to fade quickly.

In my experience, delight is very subtle. It is not a fireworks display. Rather it is the gentleness of morning dew slowly running off the tree leaf. It is the sunset that takes our breath away.

Delight is another function or expression of Awakeness. Delight is the happiness we experience when encountering unconditioned truth—the truth of the Absolute—that whatever is conditioned is subject to birth, decay, and death, and whatever is unconditioned has always been, and will eternally be, in existence.

Delight is often experienced as an uplifting internal buoyancy when encountering the unconditioned or engaging Absolute aspects. It is the happiness that arises instantaneously and spontaneously when meeting the merged nonduality, the encompassing Oneness, of the Absolute. Relaxing the normal assertion of the self, we feel elated at the ease and unhindered, natural flow of the Absolute in life.

When first encountering the quality of delight, I found I held an overall distrust for everything because I mistrusted adults as a child. I then projected this mistrust onto the Absolute, which caused me to reject experiences of delight as unreliable or even fake. In addition to this sense of mistrust, I also felt undeserving of delight to the point where I actively rejected it as unmerited.

With repeated contact, though, my resistances and sense of unworthiness softened. My old story of me began to slowly change and shift toward greater openness, a willingness to be curious.

Curiosity helps us avoid being complacent about the delight of the Absolute. Curiosity also has a learning edge to it. It holds the perspective that we do not know all that can be gleaned from an experience. There is always more to unpack, to be revealed.

Delight Exercise

What is your understanding of your delight?

When are you naturally in contact with delight?

What prevents you from opening to your delight?

What would life look like if you opened more fully to delight?

UNIFICATION

THROUGH OUR NORMAL human lens of me, we see the dualistic world with a binary view of me and not me. The life objective of the me is to get everything we desire and to reject or avoid everything we see as unwanted or not me. We try to connect with whatever we see as beneficial for the continuation of the me.

The benefit to the me is the normal human orientation. What's in it for me? This viewpoint is narrowly focused, fixated even, on personal benefit. We are not concerned with the benefit to others. It is a kind of desperate hoarding of experience.

By focusing on the benefits to the me, we close off from the subtlety being revealed slowly by the Absolute. By opening our focus from me to us, we include more of Absolute reality and align with the subtle flows and currents of the Absolute in consciousness.

With the viewpoint of unification, we are seeing all of reality, including ourselves, as a singular expression of an undivided whole. We witness the fabric of Oneness, how the Absolute actually functions and presents. We hunger for connection and union. We orient toward solidarity and union with the Absolute, longing to return home. Through repeated expressions and experiences of unification, we begin to recognize what is already united in Oneness. In contacting this ever-present Oneness, we feel more relaxed and at peace. We can truly rest.

My contact with unification was difficult at first. I simply did not feel connected to much, other than myself. I saw myself as a solitary entity maneuvering through life, trying to grasp and hold whatever felt essential to my survival. I had tunnel vision on the me rather than a wider view of an us.

Through meditation, my sense of self softened. I began to feel an us in my meditation and began to behold this in the world. I began to witness how my actions and attitude impacted others. Working the Zen pure precept of "Do good for others" allowed me to see beyond my defenses. The contraction of the me allowed and invited awareness to expand beyond my personal space.

Unification Exercise

What is your understanding of your experience of unification?

When are you naturally in contact with unification?

What prevents you from opening to unification?

What would life look like if you opened more fully to unification?

BEINGNESS

THE COUNTERPOINT TO Beingness is orientation toward the self. When we are focused exclusively on our own experiences and reflections, we are closing off to the flow of the Absolute. Beingness is about expansive wholeness. It includes witnessing the wholeness in the mundane. Much as each part of a hologram contains the whole, the fullness of Being is reflected in any minute expression of everyday, conditioned reality.

For many of us, Beingness is intimidating. It is much like staring into the grandeur of wilderness or natural beauty. We often prefer to turn away from the magnitude of Being to hold dear the self's relationship to what is witnessed. We choose to turn our view from the fullness of the entire whole to a small beneficial piece of the whole. This is safer and does not require us to take the risk of easing our grip on control.

Beingness is another way to refer to the Presence of the Absolute. When we talk about Presence, we are talking about contacting a hereness, a nowness, in our experience or perception. The quality of Beingness gives a little more dimensionality to the Presence of the Absolute. It conveys an aliveness, a fluid receptivity and welcome activity. It has a deep thoroughgoing acceptance quality to it. Beingness is also opening to the optimistic generativeness of the Absolute.

When first contacting Beingness, I was suspicious. I puzzled over whether I was feeling an expansive Beingness or just imagining it. I was distrustful. Yet the presence of Beingness persisted. It was objective and not affected by my mistrust and suspicion. As Beingness persisted in my meditation and slowly entered my daily life, I began to sense and feel the underlying flow animating all life. I was able to witness Beingness, particularly in nature. Spending increasing time in nature allowed me to soften my resistances and open to a deeper contact with, and acceptance of, Beingness.

Beingness Exercise

What is your understanding of your Beingness?

When are you naturally in contact with Beingness?

What prevents you from opening to your Beingness?

What would life look like if you opened more fully
to Beingness?

NONCONCEPTUAL PERCEPTION

MOST PERCEPTION IS conceptual perception: We see an object. We have yet to identify this object. First, we determine whether it is good for me, bad for me, or neutral to me. As we begin to identify the object being perceived, we draw up associations, memories, history, and ideas about the particular object. We connect to our past life stories related to the object or the perceived reality of the object. Our labels and comments on our experience identify the object and help us relate it to the sense of me.

There is comfort in keeping the world well defined and well organized or controlled. We then know what is happening and how it relates to our life. This gives us comfort by avoiding any contact with the mystery of the Absolute.

To open to nonconceptual perception, we slowly and deliberately challenge this belief in our ability to control life. We incrementally open to the unknown, the mystery of the Absolute. We let the me soften. Learning to have direct experiences without a sense of me or any conceptual labels is an important part of Buddhist paths of Awakening.

With nonconceptual perception, we contact each newly perceived object with natural curiosity and "not knowing." We wonder, we ponder, without falling into a routine knowing of this new object. We welcome the function of not knowing, or "Great Doubt" as we refer to it in the Zen tradition. When thoughts, mental associations, and conceptual stories commence, we keep orienting toward a deeper, nonconceptual point or place of contact in response.

We know when we are contacting the nonconceptual because our ideas, stories, life history, and mental associations quiet. They fall away. Awareness remains in contact with the object while seemingly experiencing the object from the inside facing outward. We experience the perceived object from its deepest expression and its known meaning rather than from our conceptual projections.

Feeling and sensing into nonconceptual perception was unnerving for me at first. I had never been without my thoughts, preferences, memories, and opinions. I was most comfortable in a world of words and ideas rather than a world of direct experience.

Holding fast to words and concepts gave me comfort. I felt I fit into my familiar and manageable conceptual world then. However, with meditation time and experience, I was able to occasionally drop beneath my resistance and feel the nonconceptual stream beneath the world of thoughts and words. This nonconceptual stream felt more directly real, more authentic, than my world of ideas, words, and concepts.

Nonconceptual Perception Exercise

What is your understanding of nonconceptual perception?

When are you naturally in contact with nonconceptual perception?

What prevents you from opening to nonconceptual perception?

What would life look like if you opened more fully to nonconceptual perception?

TENDERNESS

ANOTHER WORD FOR the quality of tenderness could be "suppleness." In contrast, much of our personality orients toward rigidity and positional fixedness. Our personality really does not welcome change. Whatever is predictable and routine is safe. Whatever is unknown or undefined raises a suspicion that we may be in some form of danger.

In the deepening of Awakeness, we slowly relax our tightly held beliefs and definitions of the world around us. This relaxation allows small moments where we perceive phenomena directly without our typical labels and history. We see nature as nature sees itself.

Tenderness is a soft, responsive resilience. It has a strong flexibility to it. This means the Absolute can be soft and receptive without surrendering inner fortitude and unmatched strength. Tenderness allows us to be more intimate with our personality patterns, our stories of me, and our strong preferences for like and dislike, without completely identifying. Tenderness also supports us in being more open and amenable to the *dukkha*, the discomfort or suffering, in ourselves and others.

Opening to and applying tenderness to our life allows a softening, an opening to happen. We begin to intentionally reveal to ourselves our deepest hurts and wounds. Interestingly, as we open more fully to authentic tenderness, to greater vulnerability, we also open further to the heart and love qualities and functions of the Absolute.

This tenderness is one of spirit and spiritual technique. We are softening to our inner sense of reality while testing our story of me for truth. Additionally, we are able to invite deepening tenderness to our meditation and spiritual practices. In Buddhism—and Zen in particular—the more subtle and tender our spiritual practice becomes, the more potent and life-changing the insight or understanding. We can train ourselves to meet very difficult life challenges by opening gently to tenderness. This allows us to see more deeply into our inner emotional and psychological wounding as well as to open to the loving support and deep, thoroughgoing acceptance of the Absolute.

When I first encountered tenderness, I saw it as weakness, as vulnerability. Clearly, I felt it was something to avoid. Vulnerability meant to me that I was being exposed to likely ridicule and rejection. By presenting a tough impenetrable exterior self-image, I believed I could prevent hurt and rejection. This was patently untrue. The more tender I became, the deeper my connections with others were. Life became more meaningful as I began operating on a subtler, softer, more pliant level of reality.

Tenderness Exercise

What is your understanding of your tenderness?

When are you naturally tender?

What prevents you from opening to your tenderness?

What would life look like if you opened more fully to tenderness?

FLOW

FLOW IS A MOVEMENT, a current of wisdom and deep, intuitive knowing. It is one way to describe the generative function of the Absolute.

Contraction and constriction are the worldly opposites of flow. We can create inner walls and other types of constriction to protect ourselves. We often feel if we are significantly open, we are extremely vulnerable to hurt. This applies also to our tendency to compartmentalize our experiences. Whatever feels safely contained is not at risk of being lost. Yet these very walls of seeming protection simultaneously block our contact with the subtle flow of the Absolute.

To abide in the flow quality of Awakeness, we have to deeply trust the movement and the wisdom of the Absolute. As we develop and deepen our trust in the Absolute and in our true nature, we feel safer opening to the subtle flow of the Absolute. By opening more deeply to the flow quality of Awakeness, we are putting down our impulse to control all aspects of our life and beginning to trust in the benevolence of the Absolute. In truth, we are, and always will be, taken care of as is most appropriate and beneficial for our circumstances.

The Absolute also does not maintain or measure time. It is always now and here. It took me a number of years to find a term to describe how the Absolute updates and modifies as it expands in wisdom. I now use the term "generative" to describe this ability and quality of change of beneficial adaptation. The function of generativeness is flow.

After completing Zen dharma transmission with my teacher Mark Sando Mininberg, Roshi, I found I could sense and align with the flow, the current, of the realization of the past lineage Zen teachers, the people whose realizations contributed to the generative function of the Absolute. Sensing this flow, this particular current, allowed me to feel the movement and direction of teaching in all its various applications.

Flow Exercise

What is your understanding of flow in your spiritual and/or meditative practice?

When are you naturally in contact with flow?

What prevents you from opening to the subtle flow of the Absolute?

What would life look like if you opened more fully to the flow of the Absolute?

PURITY

NORMALLY WHEN WE speak about purity, we include its positional opposite, impurity. We customarily see what is dirty or unclean in life as impure. But the purity of the Absolute does not reject what is dirty or unclean as impure. Impurity is a conceptual judgment. The term "impurity" does not actually reveal the inner quality of dirty water, for example.

When we contact the Absolute's purity, it is typically first in meditation. There can be a perception of a brightness, a brilliant lightness, in this manifest function of the Absolute. When encountering brilliantly bright purity, we can initially feel overwhelmed by our perceived historic unworthiness. Purity can trigger an emotional and psychological contraction of unworthiness. We feel we are not good enough, pure enough, to abide in direct contact with the Absolute's purity. These feelings of unworthiness plague most people.

The Absolute's purity is the freshness, the bright light, of deep, thoroughgoing acceptance and authentic respect for all expressions of the Absolute. This purity is the originality of the Absolute. It is like a clear mountain stream that flows with freshness and a crystal clarity. Yet when it enters a nearby city, the clean mountain water can be directed through a dirty city canal. This is how we can explain the horrific acts humans can do to each other. It is the purity of the Absolute corrupted by the historic pollutants of suspicion and mistrust.

As we deepen our contact with the Absolute, we slowly learn to trust it. Additionally, this is where working with a realized teacher is essential. We each need a teacher whom we have confidence in and can trust wholeheartedly to guide us and, most importantly, validate and confirm our experiences of and with the Absolute.

By deepening our innate goodness and *mettā* (unborn love) meditation practices on and off the cushion, we learn to recognize and accept our goodness unshackled to our actions or behavior. The Absolute's love can be differentiated into innate goodness, unborn love, and more. These qualities and functions do not insist we meet or accept them. They are available to contact and use when we are ready to accept their proximity in our consciousness and being.

As we increasingly accept the Absolute's purity in our experience and lives, we begin to see more readily the purity of our being and actions as well as the untarnished purity of others in their being and actions. We orient to witnessing the purity of the Absolute more often. This increases our truth of, and in, the Absolute, which increasingly confirms our direct contact.

When I first encountered the purity of the Absolute, I felt distrustful. I did not want to accept or acknowledge the purity. I was convinced it was not true, not available to me, and would be withdrawn from me soon. By slowly testing it to make sure it was safe and stable, I was able to open more and more fully to the Absolute's purity.

Purity Exercise

What is your understanding of your purity?

When are you naturally in direct contact with the purity of the Absolute?

What prevents you from opening to the Absolute's purity?

What would life look like if you opened more fully to the purity of the Absolute?

ALONENESS

Many of us take solace and comfort in the company of others. Humans seem to be pack animals, gravitating to feeling safest with others, where we may feel seen and supported. Many find solace in deep personal one-on-one relationships. Others find comfort in groups and social engagements. Being in company is part of our technique and strategy to avoid aloneness.

Aloneness is the direct experience of having nothing to hide behind or lean on. It is the willingness to be revealed and uncovered in the spotlight of truth and potent Presence of the Absolute. We need to cultivate and develop a relationship with aloneness. Until we can be deeply comfortable with aloneness, we cannot abide deeply in the emptiness, the nothingness, the Absence, the unmanifest functioning of the Absolute. Aloneness is necessary if we are to orient toward and open to being absorbed into the core, the source, of the Absolute—Cessation.

When the awareness of our meditation practice opens into the Absolute, we often experience a vast void of space. It feels and appears as an unlimited, unending spaciousness. This unlimited, unbounded space is unnerving, deeply unsettling, at first blush. We feel tiny in this neutral, objective expanse of openness.

If we are not comfortable with aloneness, we can feel it as isolation, which we experience as a sense of being abandoned. This feeling of abandonment supports our perception of our unworthiness. We simply distrust anything or anyone who offers to trust us. We feel something must be wrong with the Absolute or the other person extending the welcoming hand of trust to us.

We can also struggle with aloneness in *jhāna* practice, where a meditator often first tries to open to an unbound experience of no sense of self or thought. Our inherent survival instinct activates and then anchors us to a sudden halt. We fear that entering this territory without a customary me or any thoughts is equivalent to death. This fear of death or extinction is the strongest restraint that keeps us terrestrial practitioners rooted in our conceptual world of self-identity. We cannot leave the gravitational pull of our identity without contacting and deeply experiencing the Absolute's love, Presence, and peace. We must know with each cell of our body that the Absolute is truly our home, our birthplace to rest comfortably in aloneness.

There have been many times when I have encountered aloneness in my practice life. At first aloneness was frightening to me. I felt exposed and vulnerable, with no control of the situation. This led to the contraction and collapse of my desire to simply be in the fullness of the Absolute.

But slowly I drew back my cloak of protection to reveal my vulnerability to the Absolute. Rather than being exposed in shame, I found freedom, liberation even. I could trust the Absolute. This supported my continued opening and exposing of my vulnerabilities. In time, my vulnerability became my protection against the risk of being fully exposed. Abiding in full vulnerability let me witness that whenever a situation arose that previously would have felt risky, I did not need to feel concern. The potential injury to me was vanquished through my openness and willingness to be completely exposed.

Aloneness Exercise

What is your understanding of your aloneness?

What is your reaction to the prospect of aloneness?

What prevents you from opening to aloneness?

What would life look like if you opened more fully to aloneness?

SURRENDER

OUR LIFE HISTORY contains a plethora of experiences confirming that risking new highs or dredging up past lows increase our suffering. Each human society advertises many ways we can avoid the hazards of risky highs and be protected from new crushing lows. Some societies discourage exploration of the edges of reality, in effect, encouraging us to stay within the limits of our dysfunctions. We are taught to pull back from newness, where life has reinforced that the possibility of failure lurks.

Surrender is often associated with losing or giving up. Our resistance to surrender shows up as maintaining a tight grip on our perceptions and beliefs about the world we live in. In other words, we believe that the more tightly we hold on to our beliefs and convictions about who we are and how the world works, the happier and more successful we will be. This means we project our worldview and self-view onto our existence, hoping and expecting everyone else will agree with our perceptions and beliefs and mirror those back to us.

Ironically, it is only when we begin to surrender our grip upon our belief in consensual reality that we begin to experience truth. Truth is always slightly outside our opinions and convictions. In Zen, roshis will typically point to the unconditioned reality of the Absolute through their words and gestures. An admonition accompanies these words and actions: "Do not take the finger pointing to the moon as the moon."

On our meditation journey, we need to be willing to ascend new highs and dredge up unspeakable lows. To truly surrender is to completely let go of all manner and aspects of control. We must release our need to be the sole driving force of our life. We must trust.

We start slowly with surrender, by softening our control just briefly. We expect something bad to happen, but nothing does. We try to soften and release a little more of our projected reality. If our surrender is appropriately timed, we will feel the force of the Absolute enter and provide the support we need. We will have the vision and strength to accept life without the self controlling our experience.

As a practice, we need to learn new skills and cultivate new experiences in new territories of the Absolute. We do this through sincere surrender, meaning we hold nothing back in our radical acceptance of our new experience. Sincere, heartfelt surrender is the only way to fully land in a new experience. We cannot place conditions on it or get the Absolute to bend to our personal will and guarantee an easy experience. Surrender is profoundly tied to our level of trust in receiving teaching and to our deepest heartfelt aspiration for deep and full Awakening.

When I was initially called to surrender, I resisted. Letting go completely felt risky and foolish. I was convinced of society's view that I was the master of my own destiny. Unless I completely invested in an activity, I would never secure the results I desired.

I discovered that the deeper my authentic surrender, my giving up of my world and self-views, the more contact I had with the Absolute. I found I began to have a more open and inclusive view of myself and the world. I began to notice the important subtlety of the Absolute's appearance and functioning as everyday life. Rather than feeling weak and powerless, I was in touch with the potency, the powerful force of stillness and love, of the Absolute. My life began to work more smoothly with less frustration and anger. My relationships improved with little conscious effort.

Surrender Exercise

What is your understanding of your spiritual surrender?

When are you naturally in contact with surrender?

What prevents you from opening to your surrender?

What would life look like if you opened more fully to surrender?

SERVICE

A PERSON DEEPLY committed to the story of me is often quite closed to other possibilities. Their individual needs are paramount. The self needs so much support and comfort that they become numb to the suffering, the needs, of others. It is a me-first orientation.

This self-preoccupation applies to both spiritual and secular life. It is a fervent focus on getting more from the world and from our spiritual practices. We want to hoard the good experiences in our life.

The main block to being authentically of service is a lack of humility, a kind of spiritual conceit. It is an experience where the egoic structures exercise dominion and possession over all spiritual experience. This is maintained by our allegiance to putting the me first over all else. We try desperately to avoid discomfort and accumulate pleasant experiences. We try to "bank" the desirable, hoping that others will see our collection of beneficial experiences as a confirmation of our worthiness. We do all of this to counteract the messaging we feel emanating from our core wound saying that we are irreversibly broken and forever damaged.

As contact with the Absolute deepens through engaging transformational personality work and penetrating transcendent experience of the Absolute, we begin to feel and witness the difficulties, the *dukkha*, of an average human life. We see the immense suffering of the world that had previously been out of sight due to our preoccupation with ourselves.

Should spiritual conceit arise, we want to first acknowledge its appearance. It is here. Being with our spiritual conceit allows it to soften a little. This softening will allow our awareness to begin inhabiting the conceit while peeling back the layers of self-identity's ownership of spiritual experience. We can then release our possessiveness of our spiritual experience of attainment and orient toward authentic humility, the true meaning of service. With authentic humility, we can see that the world's suffering is our suffering.

The Absolute is objectively neutral. It loves each being equally and unrestrictedly, and its flow or current is one of inclusion. Rather than evaluating all beings and choosing ones who have high potential for deep Awakening, the Absolute shares itself equally and fully with all. It views each of us as important functioning pieces of the whole. The deeper our Awakening, the greater our gratitude and willingness to be of service to the Absolute.

For some, being of service means being an Awakening teacher, supporting students on the arduous journey of shedding their binding self-beliefs and opening to the freedom and expanse of the unending Absolute. I view my function as a teacher of Sōtō and Rinzai Zen and Theravada Buddhism as an expression of service. Certainly, the easiest path for me would be to simply focus on deepening my own path and practice.

Others will find their calling in some other expression of service. Any vocation that is uplifting and beneficial to others is a viable offering of service. When we can witness others as ourself, when we can give freely and heartfully in whatever expression we are offering, we are being of service.

As a beginning teacher, I felt great humility and a certain measure of insecurity. When I was deeply invested in my teaching insecurity, I was unable to rest in authentic humility. As I gained some confidence that I was presenting the teaching from an authentic experiential understanding and that my primary motivation was gratitude for my teachers preserving and sharing these ancient practices, I began to land in authentic service.

Service Exercise

What is your understanding of service?

When are you naturally in contact with service?

What prevents you from offering yourself in service to the Absolute?

What would life look like if you opened more fully to being of service to the Absolute?

PART II

The Roots of Awakeness

> *To fully understand what we are orienting toward after our Awakening, we need to reflect on the source of all reality, all manifestation—the Absolute.*

THE ABSOLUTE

WE EACH NEED experiential knowledge of the qualities and functions of Awakeness to cultivate, develop, and integrate these important qualities into consciousness. But to fully understand what we are orienting toward after our Awakening, we need to reflect on the source of all reality, all manifestation—the Absolute. As I have experienced and teach Awakening, it begins and ends with the Absolute, the alpha and omega of reality.

It's fundamental that we understand, at least conceptually, how reality functions. To do so from a Buddhist perspective means understanding the relationship of the Absolute to the relative, the unconditioned to the conditioned. (The terms Absolute and the unconditioned are synonymous, as are the relative and conditioned reality.)

The Absolute is used to mean Absolute reality or Absolute truth. The Absolute is the source of all manifestation and creation. It is and always has been here, right now. Being unborn, the Absolute is without any condition of existence; that is, it is unconditioned. "Unborn" means it does not have a birth, decay, or death. It has been and always will be in existence.

The relative or conditioned reality is always dependent. It depends upon other beings for its life and very existence. Once born or created, it begins to immediately grow and decay. Death is an intertwined part of life for all that is conditioned.

Most people in the world take conditioned reality, including their perception of a self, a me, as ultimate or foundational reality. But while the conditioned world is an expression of the Absolute, it is not the Absolute in all expressions. Instead, the Absolute and the relative share an interwoven coexistent reality. The conditioned or relative reality is dependent upon the Absolute for its continued existence. Without the unborn, undying quality or functions of unconditioned reality, the possibility and power of peace and love to manifest in awareness in our lives would be missing.

The Absolute has two primary functions: the manifest and the unmanifest. The manifest contains the functioning of pure love, pure Presence, and pure awareness. For those meditators with inner sight, it will appear brilliantly white. This is because the closest color we have to this brilliant brightness is white, but in truth, it is not white but rather all colors combined.

The unmanifest, conversely, contains the functioning of deep peace, primal stillness, and vast Absence (called "emptiness" in traditional Buddhism). The unmanifest appears to visual meditators as a vast, expansive, luminous darkness. Although the closest color we have is black, the unmanifest Absolute is actually without any color, resembling a very dark colorlessness.

At the core of the Absolute is a process, a potential unifying experience that we call Cessation in Buddhism. It is the ending of all materiality and mentality. Let yourself imagine what the lack of all materiality—meaning all physicality—and the lack of all mentality—meaning all mental functioning, including thoughts and concepts to define or categorize our world and experience—would be like. As well, the experience of Cessation includes a silencing of the sense of self we all carry.

Cessation is experienced by orienting toward rooted peace, deep-seated Absence, and the profound stillness of the unmanifest Absolute. When peace and stillness combine with Absence, these qualities have the capacity and function of unrestrained, thoroughgoing acceptance. This means when the meditator approaches Cessation, thoughts slow and stop; all markers of identity, of a me, disappear.

As the markers of our identity start to fade, the final two psychological functions that we experience are awareness and consciousness. As consciousness and awareness move deeper into Cessation, consciousness quiets and stops. We then are functioning as and with pure awareness. Pure awareness means awareness without reflective conceptual capability. We cannot compare what is in perception with any memory or prior experience. It is new and fresh. Pure awareness softens as it meets the deep, unending peace and embracing, inclusive stillness, until it too ceases.

And then there is nothing. In deep Cessation there is no awareness, no perception of nothingness. It is like a dreamless, deep sleep. The body relaxes deeply in its place. The mind is silent. Identity is nowhere.

Abiding in deep Cessation reboots, refreshes, and rejuvenates. One marker of true Cessation is the refreshed Awakeness that appears upon Awakening from it. This quality of refreshed Awakeness is evident after all deep Awakening experiences. Awakening from Cessation feels as though we are arising from the most enriching, nourishing, satisfying sleep of our lives. Spending minutes or hours steeping in Cessation orients us toward the ultimate truth of Cessation: It is the center and driving force of the Absolute and, hence, of all reality.

In the Theravada Buddhist tradition, as I learned it, post-Cessation is the key to all Awakening experiences. Abiding in Cessation resets our view of reality and our self-identity. Following a deep Cessation experience, or any deep Awakening experience such as *kenshō*, there is a period of understanding and integration, where the fruits of the experience will first be witnessed. We can then intentionally make changes to have our outer world more accurately reflect, reveal, and support our inner one. We can begin living our Awakeness.

OUR BUDDHA NATURE

THE BUDDHA'S GREAT Awakening experience formed the foundation for all of Buddhism. He systematized existing meditation practices into a sequence that leads to the progressive deconstruction of our belief in and allegiance to the customary sense of self. This is the path of gradual purification of mind—a purification of self.

These sequential practices have been carefully preserved in Theravada Buddhism. (In my book *Liberating the Self*, I present the entirety of the samadhi, or concentration, practices taught by the Buddha.) In addition, the Buddha's personal path of purification of mind and realization of the Absolute has also supported the Zen/Chan/Son[1] teachings and practices, resulting in its unbroken lineage of transmitting the light of Awakening.

In a seeming individual consciousness, the various qualities of the Absolute realm are called "Buddha nature" or "true nature." That is, our true nature is entirely composed of the

---

1   Son is a Korean Zen tradition.

Absolute inhabiting all consciousness. Becoming a Buddha means maturing and dropping our complete identity with body or mind while the Absolute awakens to itself in consciousness as a foundation—a core for deep intuitive knowing, wholesome understanding, and wise action. A Buddha is one for whom the sense of self has fallen away, and the flow of Awakeness guides and informs their perception, actions, and expression of reality. This is also called a *Daigo-tettei* realization, meaning "full or final enlightenment," or *tathāgata*, meaning "thus come, thus gone." The Buddha is also known as Tathāgata.

To align with our Buddha nature as the guide for our Awakeness, we need to remind ourselves what that nature entails. Two anchors hold us: the *trikaya* (the three manifestation bodies of a Buddha), and the nine attributes of a Buddha. These markers orient us to potentially attaining, embodying, and expressing Buddhahood in this lifetime as practiced and lived by the Buddha.

Trikaya

The *trikaya* is one way of understanding and witnessing the potential full flowering of our realization. It was developed to allow both the Theravada and Mahayana practitioners to revere and admire the Buddha while not undermining their philosophical framing of Buddhism.

Tri means "three" and *kaya* means "body" or "bodies"—the three bodies of the reality of a Buddha. These three bodies, or expressive functions, are the *dharmakaya*, *sambhogakaya*, and *nirmanakaya*, which represent an awake *tathāgata* or Buddha.

We all have these three functions of a *tathāgata*, but most people are not in direct contact with them. We can align with our Buddha nature by getting in touch with the *trikaya*.

Dharmakaya: The Truth Body

Dharmakaya is another name for the realization and embodiment of the Absolute in a particular consciousness. The *dharmakaya* is the Buddha's reality expressed as a truth body or Absolute/cosmic body. It is the source of all spiritual and meditative practices, including the *brahmavihāras* (the ancient heart practices). Interestingly, the initial *kōans* in formal study are referred to as *dharmakaya kōans*.

Sambhogakaya: The Bliss Body

This Buddha reality appearing as a bliss body focuses on the enjoyment of being in this body that is not overly affected by human conditions, unconscious patterns, and well-worn proclivities. *Sambhogakaya* is particularly enjoying resting in and as the Absolute, knowing it is the Absolute. Love is known and directly experienced as all reality and every location. The *sambhogakaya* is a fulfillment of the Absolute perceiving itself and acting from that inclusive perception.

Resting in and as the *sambhogakaya* leads to a reduced fear of death or extinction.

Nirmanakaya: The Physical Body

This is the Buddha reality appearing as an emanation body, the one made of the four elements (earth, water, fire, and wind) and subject to old age, sickness, and death. With a deep understanding of the *trikaya*, we can know that this *nirmanakaya* must succumb to sickness, old age, and death despite the reality that the *dharmakaya* does not die or become infirm. The temporality of this physical body is also experienced in the ordinary bliss of being human.

Nine Attributes of a Buddha

Another method we can employ to confirm the full realization of being a functioning *tathāgata* is to apply the following nine attributes of a Buddha to our consciousness:

1 No defilements
2 Perfect enlightenment
3 Direct knowing of and maintaining *sīla*
4 Right speech
5 Knowledge of other realms
6 Soothing of others' turmoil
7 Teacher to those seen and unseen
8 Awake
9 Good karma

No Defilements

In traditional Buddhism, three major defilements cloud the clarity and light of the Absolute: desire, aversion, and delusion.

Desire is that part of our personality that wants things. Some of our wants, such as food, water, and shelter, are basic to our survival. But our desires beyond survival necessities are what support a separate personality. We may feel that unless we get a certain work position, possession, or relationship, we will not feel whole or complete; we will feel less than others. The desire defilement is the inner driver of deficiency that propels us to seek that thing that will help us feel whole and complete.

As you know from life experience, once we get this elusive object, it rarely extinguishes our feelings of inner deficiency. Soon the deficiency is activated again when we see someone possess something that makes them appear content and happy. "If I can only get that, I will be satisfied and feel complete," we think. This is the compulsive draw of the desire defilement.

Aversion is the rejection of whatever is appearing in life that we actively do not want. The motivation of the aversion defilement is to keep bad things away to allow only the positive, good, happy experiences to be close to us. With aversion, we must maintain an inner radar to assess what is beneficial and what is harmful, a constant exercise of judgment as to what is good and what is bad. This requires a lot of energy and constant judging of the world as it is appearing.

The delusion defilement exists until we experience a deep Awakening. This primary delusion is the firm belief in the concept of a me. Our families and societies model the purported reality that we are each a separate individual whose efforts alone determine the outcome of a life of joy or suffering. This delusion compounds as we begin to also believe we make things happen. We invest in the belief of cause and effect.

In reality, there is no actor and no action that results in a particular effect. From the perspective of realization, there are simply separate actions that happen in a wisdom that is unfolding exactly as needed. We each have free will to make choices and change the course of our lives. Are our seeming choices creating a result? Or might the result have happened regardless of our efforts or desires?

As we can see, none of the defilements are ultimately beneficial. They are psychological or personality strategies to keep us as safe and happy as possible. The problem is that valuing and chasing these defilements as a life strategy invites greater disharmony. We are constantly reaching for something we do not have but desperately want. Even if we see through and liberate ourselves from these dysfunctional patterns of personality, they can still continue to operate on a subtle level.

Deeply awakened, the *tathāgata* or Buddha is not yoked to these defilements. They can feel the gentle pull of the defilements without needing to succumb to their dysfunctional application. As we develop or mature our Buddha nature, a variety of memories and compulsions can and will arise spontaneously after deep Awakening. These arise because they are incongruent with the impact of the deep Awakening. We do not seek or expect to eliminate these memories and patterns of behavior. Rather we learn to work with each of these defilements as it arises without succumbing to the historic draw or pull of a distant egoic dysfunction.

Perfect Enlightenment

To be recognized as a *tathāgata* or Buddha requires the Zen Awakening of *Daigo-tettei*, the Great or Final Awakening. We reach the final realization that the self-identity has always been thoroughly absent, and we gain complete union with the Absolute. There is never a time or experience where the *tathāgata* is out of contact with the Absolute. The Absolute is always the inner experience of reflection.

We shift from "I am experiencing the Absolute" to "The Absolute is experiencing itself in this particular location." As we work through the lingering yet fading personality patterns, we feel less like an individual and more a particular expression of the Absolute. We understand that the Absolute is functioning as us.

Direct Knowing of and Maintaining *Sīla*

The *tathāgata* is not monitoring their behavior to keep in accord with the flow or current of the Absolute. Rather the *tathāgata* is oriented toward the Zen pure precept "Do good for others." "Others" refers to all beings, including the body of the *tathāgata*. Simply, we align with conduct that benefits the majority of beings—that is, *sīla* or wholesome behavior and actions. Concurrently the *tathāgata* also watches for openings where the Absolute can be introduced to a student in a manner that is impactful or slightly startling. This can spark a no-self, unity, or *kenshō* experience in the student.

The Buddhist precepts are the guides toward and expressions of awakened behavior. As a *tathāgata*, we will maintain the precepts with minimal effort. It is simply the natural, obvious way to behave. Our default is to be of benefit while radiating an offer of goodness to all beings, always.

Right Speech

Right speech in traditional Theravada Buddhism suggests avoiding idle speech, gossip, and divisive speech. The *tathāgata* orients always toward the innate goodness of the Absolute manifesting in each being. The tenderness in our heart is in perfect union with all beings everywhere, always. Accordingly, we speak in a unifying manner, including all and excluding none.

Knowledge of Other Realms

A *tathāgata* understands that the *kōan* "Ordinary mind is the way" does not mean that the usual mindstream of the average person on the planet is the same as a *tathāgata's* mindstream. The *tathāgata* will have what we might call "ordinary mind." Yet for the *tathāgata* there is no identification with the workings of "ordinary mind."

By softening and dropping the steadfast allegiance to the conceptual world and its definitions, we begin to contact and abide in the nonconceptual realms. Other realms include the upper or formless *jhānas* of Theravada Buddhism: the Base of Boundless Space, the Base of Boundless Consciousness, the Base of No-thing-ness, and the Base of Neither Perception nor Nonperception, among others.

Soothing of Others' Turmoil

When we are a *tathāgata*, we have a magnanimous heart-flow. We perceive no separation between ourselves and any other beings; we are an indivisible Oneness of differentiated Absolute.

All dissatisfaction and suffering in the world in each breath is felt and heard by the *tathāgata*. In perceiving this worldly suffering, the *tathāgata* sees no response other than opening the Absolute heart wider to meet and relieve all beings of all suffering.

Teacher to Those Seen and Unseen

Simply walking in the world, a *tathāgata* sets forth a ripple of model behavior and unparalleled wisdom with each step taken and each word spoken aloud or silently. In effect, our silent existence alone beneficially impacts those around us. As a *tathāgata*, we teach simply by being exactly what we are—the Absolute in physical form.

Traditional Theravada Buddhism recognizes other realms, including the animal, human, hell, heaven or deva, and others. In teaching others through words, wordless words, and deep silence, the *tathāgata* cannot help but radiate the perfection of the Absolute. This radiant light of wisdom penetrates into each and every realm in deep peace and unifying Oneness. All beings, even those who are unaware of the *tathāgata*'s radiance, can sense something special is here and sense the energetic shifts that the *tathāgata*'s existence in this world affords all beings.

Awake

A *tathāgata* by nature, function, and definition is profoundly awake to the seen and unseen realities. The grand delusion that "I am exclusively a separate entity solely responsible for any life success or failure" cannot land with the *tathāgata*.

With the *Daigo-tettei* realization, the Absolute shines through like eternal morning dawn. As a *tathāgata*, we shine for all in every direction, forever emanating the bright and dark Awakeness of the Absolute, its light of wisdom radiating and illuminating the world. In perfect harmony and deep acceptance of all worldly delusions, the *tathāgata* is in perfect repose, always.

Good Karma

Karma is the universal law of cause and effect in the conditioned world, where actions appear to have consequences or results. Karma can be seen as good or bad based upon the impact on the person.

A *tathāgata* acts in complete accord with the generative functioning of the Absolute. That is, the Absolute changes and grows through a process I call "generative." It does not function in a linear fashion. The Absolute does not contain time or relative space, yet it is informed by and incorporates all realizations humans can experience.

In addition, we are in complete harmony with the Zen precepts. Accordingly, we will enjoy good karma in the relative world as a result of wholesome behavior and actions. Karma is not produced when the Absolute is functioning outside the relative world and in the pure Absolute.

Here is a *kōan* from the *Mumonkan* (*The Gateless Gate*) specifically on the issue of karma. It is Case 2 of the *Mumonkan*, "Hyakujō's Fox."

"Hyakujō's Fox"

Introduction

This is a pivotal *kōan* on the application of karma to those with confirmed Awakenings. In the Zen/Chan tradition I have heard teachers speak and act in congruence with the erroneous notion that *kenshō* releases the individual consciousness from all karmic results. But whatever is realized as the unconditioned Absolute is not subject to conditioned karma. What is conditioned in an individual (that is, subject to birth, decay, and death) remains subject to the law of karma. This error in understanding is the focus of this *kōan*.

My Translation

When Hyakujō Oshō delivered dharma *teisho* (a dharma talk, often about a particular *kōan*), an old man attended, quietly tucked in the back of the room. When the monastics filed out, the old man departed too.

One day, however, he hesitantly lingered after the monks quietly filed out of the hall, and Hyakujō asked him, "Who are you, in this moment?"

The old man responded, "I am not human, not an earth dweller. In the ancient times of Buddha Kashyapa, I was Tanto, the head of practice of this monastery.

"One day a student asked me, 'Does one experiencing *kenshō* remain yoked to cause and effect (karma)?'

"I answered, 'No, she does not.'

"Since then, I have been karmically reborn five hundred lifetimes as a fox. I beg you now to give the *hwadu*, the Absolute complete turning word. Release me from my fox lifetimes.

"Tell me—does one experiencing *kenshō* remain yoked to the world of cause and effect (karma) or not?"

Hyakujō answered, "She cannot disregard causation."

As the old man heard these words, a deep *satori/* Awakening arose.

In a deep bow, he said, "I am liberated from the karma of fox lives abiding on this mountain. Please prepare and bury my fox body as that of an attained monk."

The head monk, Hyakujō, struck the temple bell. He advised the assembly that after the noon meal there would be an attained monk's funeral.

Puzzled, the monastics stated, "Everyone is healthy. What is happening?"

Hyakujō later led the monastics to the base of a rock formation on the mountain's far side. The undergrowth revealed a fox's dead body. He performed the sacred funeral ceremony for attained monastics.

Deep in the darkness of evening he ascended the dais to explain.

Another monk, Ōbaku, thereupon asked, "The old abbot misunderstood karma and was doomed to five hundred fox rebirths. Had he offered a clear answer, what then?"

Hyakujō said, "Draw close and I will whisper the answer."

Ōbaku went up to Hyakujō and slapped him.

Hyakujō, laughing, clapped his hands and exclaimed, "I was pondering whether Bodhidharma had a red beard, but now I see Bodhidharma before me."

Mumon's Comment

Failing karma: How could this monk be reborn as a fox?
Not denying karma: How does this liberate?

When this is understood thoroughly, you will know intimately how old Hyakujō would have coped with five hundred fox rebirths.

Mugen's Comment

This is a critical *kōan* on karma. I have heard Buddhist practitioners and teachers say "everything is shadow." This suggests that since everything is Absence or Buddhist emptiness, we don't need to monitor our actions or behavior. In effect, our actions have no consequences.

Holding this viewpoint guarantees that many more lifetimes of purification and realization will be needed. Intimately understanding how karma unfolds in the conditioned world is essential. Until we know how karma arises in our own life and in the conditioned world, we will never embody the freedom of the unconditioned.

Mumon's Verse

> Not releasing, not hiding:
> Two sides of one die.
> Not hiding, not releasing:
> Unlimited errors, infinite mistakes.

Mugen's Verse

> A single raindrop in a country pond
> Creates unimaginable ripples
> Through the fabric of Now

PART III

The Theravada Path of Awakeness

> The only potential to . . . rest in what is not conditioned . . . is through the practice and experience of Awakening.

THE INITIAL TEACHING, meditations, and spiritual practices of the Buddha were first organized and presented in what we now know as Theravada Buddhism. Theravada means the "path of the elders," the traditional path likely walked by the Buddha.

Were you to arrive in this moment at my Theravada teacher's monastery, you would be given the meditation practice called *ānāpānasati*. In Pali this means "breath awareness" meditation. It is a form of meditative concentration. We undertake breath awareness meditation to begin collecting our attention and learning to consciously direct awareness to the meditative object of the breath. When we practice concentration meditation, we can potentially reach the deepest part of the third level of absorption, also called *jhāna*.

Every meditation contains the first two levels of meditative concentration: 1) momentary concentration (asking where awareness is in this moment or breath) and 2) access concentration (where awareness is beginning to access the deeper levels of concentration; experiences of joy and bliss along with mind-light phenomena occur, evidencing deepening meditative concentration).

Each level of absorption in concentration meditation practice is a very particular slice of the Absolute, the source of all reality. We are slowly and deliberately contacting and abiding in a very particular quality of the Absolute in each *jhāna* as well as in each *jhāna* factor I will describe.

Each quality of the Absolute we abide with meditatively is its own expression of Awakeness. For this reason, understanding the *jhāna* process reveals and attunes our consciousness to a particular expression of the Absolute. This understanding activates and supports this expression to more fully land in our consciousness. As these expressions of Awakeness find a home in our consciousness, we are activating our true nature.

I have written about breath awareness meditation in the book I co-authored called *Practicing the Jhānas*. Additionally, I lead retreats each year in this practice, so I will not go through all the steps of the practice here. Rather I will briefly cover the levels of meditative concentration and then focus us on the felt sense, the Awakeness qualities, of each level of absorption, each *jhāna*.

MEDITATIVE CONCENTRATION

WITHIN THE MULTITUDE of possible meditations, there are two groups of meditation: concentration meditation and all other meditations.

Concentration meditation is categorized as such because it has an unchanging meditation object. The meditation object is the primary focus. For example, in breath awareness meditation (*ānāpānasati*), the sole and exclusive meditative object is the breath crossing the *ānāpāna* region, between the nostrils and upper lip. There is never another meditative object in this type of concentration meditation.

There are three levels available in concentration meditations:

1 Momentary concentration

2 Access concentration

3 Absorption concentration/*jhāna*

Momentary Concentration

Momentary concentration is simply asking, "Where is awareness in this breath, this moment?" Our sole function at this stage of concentration meditation is to keep returning awareness to the meditative object. Awareness begins to settle and rest on the meditative object.

Once awareness can be maintained for ten to fifteen minutes without serious interruption, I would consider the student to be in the second level of meditative concentration—access concentration.

Access Concentration

Access concentration is called access because it is close to accessing the third level of meditative concentration called absorption or *jhāna*.

One of the markers of access concentration is awareness regularly resting on the meditative object with minimal effort on our part. Simply put, there is greater ease and stability in the meditation.

In addition, qualities of the unconditioned Absolute begin to appear in access concentration. These are called the *jhāna* factors.

The *Jhāna* Factors

The *jhāna* factors appear randomly in access concentration, sometimes strongly present and other times feeling quite shallow. We do not directly influence the *jhāna* factors nor switch from the meditative object to a *jhāna* factor as our object.

The *jhāna* factors are unfortunately named. One can experience these factors deeply without reaching the third level of concentration meditation known as absorption/*jhāna*. Only when awareness is deeply concentrated and all *jhāna* factors are in full supply can *jhāna*, or absorption, be a viable potential.

The *jhāna* factors are

— *vitakka,*

— *vicāra,*

— *pīti,*

— *sukha,* and

— *ekaggatā.*

Vitakka

Vitakka is applied awareness. It is the process of returning awareness to the meditative object again and again, each time we realize our awareness is off the object.

It is particularly helpful to avoid self-blame or self-criticism when returning to the meditative object. Simply return.

Vicāra

Vicāra is sustained attention. We will have moments where awareness will rest on the meditative object. With *vicāra,* we suddenly realize that we have been resting on the breath without serious interruption for quite a while. We feel in the zone, as if our meditation is deepening, reaching into a non-ordinary reality. We are tapping into something mysterious, magical, and well outside our control.

Pīti

Pīti is bodily felt joy. With *pīti*, our physical forms feel light, delightfully happy with no seeming source of our ease and happiness. Those meditators with historic body pain, that is, those with bad backs, knees, etc., will have some physical relief, an inner lightness of ease. This body comfort invites deeper, more sustained meditation time. In effect, we can sit much longer than usual with near complete bodily ease.

Sukha

This *jhāna* factor is experienced as mental bliss. Our mind seems lightened, uplifted, almost effervescent. Concerns and worries quiet and fall away. Nothing in our experience seems to be any form of a problem or potential problem.

Ekaggatā

As we progress through the three levels of meditative concentration, our awareness refines and unifies. Rather than awareness being a wide spectrum experience, it narrows to a perceptible force, a one-pointedness, a laser-like focus—*ekaggatā*. This refined and unified awareness has the capacity and ability to penetrate more deeply into and through the meditative object. In effect, we can perceive well beyond what normal awareness can touch.

Ekaggatā becomes important as we gain the meditative concentration to penetrate our story of me, our personality allegiances, our deep conviction that my self, my personality, is a fundamental abiding reality.

As the *jhāna* factors begin to make their random appearance in access concentration, our meditation takes less effort. The *jhāna* factors invite more bodily and mental ease. We can relax a little more and let the meditation begin to do itself effortlessly. They allow us to meditate longer and longer with minimal to no discomfort or distraction.

As meditative concentration continues to deepen in access concentration, the felt sense of our body boundary, the outer edge of our body perception, will begin to soften and fall away, in part or whole. The inner felt sense of our orientation and location becomes unfocused.

In addition to the lessening or dropping of the body boundary, we can also experience the quieting of all thoughts in deep access concentration. Thoughts shift from being in close, direct perception to being like distant clouds floating across the sky of our mind. Thoughts can and will cease as meditative concentration deepens in an approach to absorption or *jhāna* meditative concentration.

Finally, our sense of a me, a self, ceases. Normally we self-reference by touching into the markers of a me. These markers include our body, thoughts, preferences, memories, emotions, beliefs, relationships, and cultural and social identity.

These all become transparent in our perception. Effectively there is no me. With no me, entering absorption/*jhāna* becomes a simple union of awareness between what has previously been viewed as "my awareness" with the awareness of the source, the Absolute. We discover there are not two awarenesses, just the Absolute awareness, seemingly segregated into universal/Absolute and personal/relative awareness.

Absorption Concentration/*Jhāna*

Interestingly, absorption suggests there is a separation, a gulf of difference, that is bridged. In fact, there has never been a separation between our awareness and Absolute awareness. Thus, absorption concentration or *jhāna* is a natural state or experience. It is returning to the Oneness, the nonduality of the Absolute. This return to the Absolute can be completed by engaging the *jhāna* practice as part of this third level of concentration meditation.

There are eight or nine *jhānas*, depending on the *jhāna* teacher or *jhāna* master's presentation. Each *jhāna* is a unique experience. The individual *jhānas* purify a particular quality of mind.

Each *jhāna* will have the flavor of the *jhāna* factors being employed for that particular one as well as the characteristics of whatever the meditative object is employed in developing deep absorption concentration. For example, breath awareness meditation would have a quality of awareness in the *jhāna*s experienced using breath.

In addition, each *jhāna* has its own energetic frequency. It is like a radio frequency, a kind of vibration or energy field. The function of *jhāna* practice is to attune our consciousness to the frequency of each *jhāna*. As each *jhāna* is a particular characteristic of the Absolute, *jhāna* practice attunes us to additional qualities of the Absolute, making our merger, our union with the Absolute, more accessible and more readily available.

Practically speaking, this means we need to abide in each *jhāna* until the energetic frequency of our consciousness perfectly matches and attunes to the energetic vibration of that particular *jhāna*.

First *Jhāna*

First *jhāna* is characterized by the attendance of all five of the *jhāna* factors. Thus, first *jhāna* will have the feel, the taste, of all applied awareness (*vitakka*), sustained awareness (*vicāra*), bodily felt joy (*pīti*), mental bliss (*sukha*), and one-pointed unified mind (*ekaggatā*). Should you imagine having these qualities as predominant in awareness, it would feel comforting, soothing even.

Experiencing the merging, the nonduality of our consciousness and the energetic rhythm of the Absolute as the qualities of first *jhāna* is deeply impactful and profound in its effects. Abiding in first *jhāna* allows our consciousness to rest in the particular Awakeness quality of first *jhāna*, which is applied awareness and sustained awareness. We are learning and developing the capacity to rest in sustained awareness, allowing the meditative process to unfold in its own ripeness.

Most yogis for whom first *jhāna* arises have a very brief first contact. Typically, a few minutes is all that can be managed and received. Initially the energetic frequency of first *jhāna* is too much for our consciousness. We are over-loaded quickly by its intensity. Over time, with repeated contact with first *jhāna*, our consciousness becomes more in harmony with its energy. As consciousness repeatedly har-monizes with first *jhāna*, the vibration of our consciousness begins to match the energetic frequency of first *jhāna*.

In time, that overwhelming first *jhāna* frequency becomes well integrated into our consciousness. Then first *jhāna* begins to feel mundane. When the yogi has a slight indifference with first *jhāna*, that is typically the sign that they are ready to approach second *jhāna*.

When a student can regularly enter and abide in first *jhāna* for an hour or more, they are usually attuned suffi-ciently to orient to second *jhāna*. If second *jhāna* does not arise after a good attempt, the student should return to first *jhāna*, increasing the time resting and abiding in first *jhāna*.

To open to the potential of second *jhāna*, the student returns to access concentration, briefly opens to first *jhāna*, then returns to first *jhāna* access concentration and focuses on the breath in the *ānāpāna* region. The student specifically focuses awareness on the last three *jhāna* factors (*pīti, sukha,* and *ekaggatā*). These three *jhāna* factors are necessary to open to second *jhāna*. When meditative concentration deepens sufficiently, in access concentration, second *jhāna* will open.

Second *Jhāna*

With the successful attunement to first *jhāna*, the yogi can now adhere to the predominant flavor or feel of second *jhāna*: the *jhāna* factors of *pīti*—bodily felt joy, *sukha*—mental bliss, and *ekaggatā*—one-pointed awareness.

Again, the yogi opens to the arising and entry into second *jhāna*. As with first *jhāna*, the energetic frequency of second *jhāna* is, initially, overwhelming. Our consciousness can accommodate only a few minutes in the stream of second *jhāna* before needing to take a break.

Second *jhāna* feels more intense than first *jhāna* despite it being a more refined, more high-pitched energy. Interestingly, in Buddhist meditation practice, the more subtle an experience is, the more potent it is likely to be.

In second *jhāna* the quality of Awakeness is *pīti*, or bodily felt joy. Experiencing *pīti* allows us to feel the joy of concentration practice as well as of experiencing union with the Absolute. With repeated merging with second *jhāna*, consciousness begins to slowly, deliberately match the energy of second *jhāna*.

When the time arises where we feel a growing neutrality to second *jhāna*, we are likely ready for third *jhāna* purification. When consciousness perfectly attunes to the energetic vibration of second *jhāna* after sufficient time resting in second *jhāna*, the yogi is ready to attempt contact with third *jhāna*.

Third *Jhāna*

In third *jhāna*, *pīti* drops, leaving two *jhāna* factors (*sukha*—mental bliss, and *ekaggatā*—one-pointed/laser-like awareness). This is a very psychologically and energetically refined experience. Experiencing subtle mental bliss together with the deep penetration of one-pointed awareness is quite impactful on our view of self and view of the world. Neither our sense of self nor the world are as we believed. Holding a viewpoint outside normal perception opens us to new vistas and heights. Third *jhāna* is a kind of milestone as it uses the most subtle *jhāna* factors as entry. When concentration gets specifically focused, we begin to deeply enjoy the ease of practice.

Third *jhāna* is both more subtle than second *jhāna* and much more potent energetically. As with the prior two *jhāna*s, initially the energy of third *jhāna* will be nearly overwhelming. It feels like being in an energetic blast furnace. It is a pure, powerful energy we are meeting. The Absolute is further purifying our mind by purifying our consciousness.

As we allow consciousness to raise its vibrations, our mind is upgrading, attuning more closely to the energetic frequency of the Absolute.

In third *jhāna*, our contact point is *sukha*, commonly translated as "mental bliss." *Sukha* is a head-only experience of effervescence, a bubbly contentment. This quality of Awakeness allows us to soften and release mental tension and lessen identity. We are deeply satisfied with intimate contact with the Absolute.

As third *jhāna* gets more comfortable and more mundane, and we attain the harmonization of energy, it is time to orient to fourth *jhāna*. One significant difference from the first three *jhānas* is that the same two *jhāna* factors are employed from fourth *jhāna* onward: established one-pointed awareness (*ekaggatā*) and a new *jhāna* factor—equanimity (*upekkhā*). Fourth *jhāna* provides the first introduction of equanimity.

Equanimity is a deep acceptance of truth. It is fully accepting what is actually occurring in this moment, in this breath, without qualification or reservation. The felt sense of equanimity's deep acceptance and of one-pointed awareness is a powerful yet subtle combination of Absolute qualities. With equanimity, the yogi accepts everything in their experience and perception. With one-pointedness, the yogi can deeply penetrate the *jhāna* and attune to the energy vibration or frequency of the *jhāna*.

From fourth *jhāna* access concentration, the yogi orients toward the *jhāna* factors of equanimity and one-pointedness. Because of the subtlety of these *jhāna* factors, the yogi may need to enter and abide deeply in first through third *jhāna* before orienting toward fourth *jhāna*.

Fourth *Jhāna*

There is a gulf between third and fourth *jhāna*. The *jhāna* factors used now become more subtle, which means meditative concentration needs to be very deep and extremely focused. This would also quiet the sense of self, the me. With no sense of self or thought, from fourth *jhāna* forward we are steeping in an unspoken truth, a deep, intuitive knowing, an experientially felt wisdom, without conceptual reference.

As awareness and consciousness focus deeply on the felt sense of equanimity and one-pointedness, there is a further refining of awareness; an inherent quality of humility arises in this territory. We understand that we are not doing any practice, nor are we attaining anything. We are returning to a natural state of mind through the *jhāna* practice. We are attuning to the Absolute's energetic qualities one by one.

In fourth *jhāna*, we are purifying and connecting with *ekaggatā*, one-pointedness. One-pointedness is a laser-like focus of awareness. This quality of Awakeness lets us have supreme focus without personal effort. This builds trust in the Absolute and confidence in our connection and ability to open and receive this deep, direct teaching of surrender.

When the yogi's consciousness has sufficiently attuned
to fourth *jhāna*, the yogi begins orienting toward fifth *jhāna*.

Formless Realms/*Jhānas*

The first four *jhānas* are referred to as "form *jhānas*" because
these are bodily felt in experience. These form *jhānas* work
to purify our mind in relation to our identity, including body
identity.

In contrast, the upper *jhānas*—the fifth through ninth
jhānas—are called the "formless *jhānas*" or "formless realms."
I prefer the term "realms" here. A realm is an experienced
location that is not subject to the laws of form such as
gravity, space, or time. In such a realm, awareness and consciousness can journey, exploring the realm and confirming
its boundaryless vastness.

The formless realms are not felt in this body. The experiential knowing in the upper *jhānas* is of awareness and consciousness moving through the top of the head, the crown
chakra in the yogic system. The reality in each of these upper/
formless realms feels very much like a kind of universe of its
own. Each realm has its own corresponding properties. For
example, the fifth *jhāna* is the Base of Boundless Space.

While steeping in each realm of the *jhāna* practice, our
consciousness harmonizes and attunes to the qualities and
functions of that realm. This acclimatizes us to that particular function of the Absolute. So when our meditative path
takes us into vast space, following attainment of the fifth

jhāna, the first formless realm, we are more at ease, more willing to abide in vast, open, boundless space with minimal reactivity or resistance.

Once consciousness and awareness experience directly the unboundedness quality of each formless realm, our tenuous hold on what we take to be reality is broken, sometimes shattered. We will never be the same. In addition, working with and through the formless realms affords us deeper, more sustained contact with these differentiated qualities of Awakeness, of the Absolute.

With sustained contact with each formless realm, we are activating this quality in our true nature. Thus, each formless realm of the Absolute informs and affects our Awakeness. As we merge completely in each formless realm with sustained contact, the realm of that particular *jhāna* is present in our consciousness, our Buddha nature, and available as a resource on the path of Awakeness.

Fifth *Jhāna*: The Base of Boundless Space

Once a yogi has spent sustained time fully merged in fourth *jhāna*, they may be ready to approach fifth *jhāna*, the first formless realm. To access the fifth *jhāna*, the yogi first needs to develop "earth *kasina*." When earth *kasina* is well established in awareness, it is present, stable, and available to engage for opening to fifth *jhāna*, the Base of Boundless Space.

Boundless space is deeply impactful. We are accustomed to limited or bound space. We routinely experience the bounded space of walls, city borders, country boundaries, even abiding on the planet Earth. Boundless space is unending space with no limitations, boundaries, or borders. As far as consciousness and awareness journey through boundless space, we find no limits of any kind. This experience helps us loosen our belief in the self contained in this particular body, in a particular area of space.

Let's look at our earth *kasina* meditation practice. (For a thorough discussion of the *kasina* practice, please see my book *Liberating the Self*.)

Earth *Kasina* Meditation Practice

- Go outside and find a patch of bare earth. It should be free of any growth, rocks, or debris.

- Using a stick, draw a circle within the patch of bare earth.

- Alternatively, you can fill a jar or pot with clean dirt with no growth or debris in it.

- Sitting near this patch of earth, view the circle intently. (Or do the same with the contents of the jar.) Really let yourself become intimate with earth. Drop beneath the conceptual knowing of earth to the deeper, nonconceptual felt sense of what earth feels like internally, intuitively.

- Let yourself feel your connection to earth, how you have earthlike qualities in your being. When humans die, their bodies begin to decay. Eventually much of this once-robust body is returned to earth, to dirt.

- Feel the softening of your beliefs in your own physical solidity. Allow the memories of your strong, solid physicality to relax to match your felt sense of nonconceptual earth—earth as something known in deep intuition rather than through memories and history.

— Let this mental picture of earth or the felt sense of the circle of earth become your sole meditative object. Invite the softening of your attachment to ideas about, or prior experiences with, the solidity of yourself or your world.

— Off the cushion, look around at all you see. What belief or story do you carry about earth? Is it a level or reality that cannot be questioned? Is it timeless?

We bring awareness to the well-established earth *kasina*. As awareness begins to merge with earth *kasina*, we orient toward the full five *jhāna* factors of first *jhāna*. We go through access concentration and into earth *kasina* first *jhāna*. Earth *kasina* first *jhāna* will have a similar felt sense to breath awareness first *jhāna* with the addition of the felt sense, nonconceptual experience of earth.

When awareness is well established in earth *kasina* first *jhāna*, we orient toward second to fourth *jhāna* as outlined above.

Once we have experienced a solid foundation in the first four form *jhānas*, we orient toward space. We can do this by orienting to the space in the pores of our skin. We can also use the opening in a keyhole or a window screen.

If we are to use earth *kasina* as our portal to fifth *jhāna*, we invite earth *kasina* to fill our awareness and experiential perception. We can either focus intently on the holes in earth *kasina* or visually hold the edges of earth *kasina* to witness and experience the space in earth *kasina*. Focusing on this space, when all is ripe, the meditation opens to fifth *jhāna*, the Base of Boundless Space.

The felt sense of fifth formless *jhāna* absorption concentration is different qualitatively than fourth *jhāna*. Instead of a bodily felt sense, awareness and consciousness exit the body through the portal of the crown chakra at the top of the head.

It is a miraculous experience for awareness and consciousness to be resting in boundless, limitless space. Awareness slowly expands into boundless space. Stretching further and further into vast space deeply impacts us, as we do not find a boundary or border. This space is truly endless.

The formless realm of boundless space puts us in direct contact with the space that holds all material reality. We are also in direct contact with the boundless space of the Absolute, a quality of Awakeness of the Absolute. Being with this quality of the Absolute lets us relax our identity in this physical body. We are completely merged, absorbed, in the vastness of space of the Absolute. These experiences of Awakeness are essential as we continue advancing through the formless realms toward potential absorption in Cessation, *Nibbāna* itself.

When the yogi experiences sustained abiding in the Base of Boundless Space for an hour or more, then they can orient toward the sixth *jhāna* and second formless realm—the Base of Boundless Consciousness.

Sixth *Jhāna*: The Base of Boundless Consciousness

As with all formless *jhānas*, we go through the sequence of establishing the first through fifth *jhānas* as we experienced these before.

When we feel solid and well-established in fifth *jhāna*, we return awareness and consciousness to fifth *jhāna*. We select a particular spot in boundless space and fixate on that spot with our awareness and consciousness. When well settled on this spot, we then orient awareness to the universal consciousness holding boundless space.

When the consciousness holding boundless space becomes a clear meditative object, we stay with that deep contact with universal consciousness, which includes our consciousness.

When we are well settled in concentration meditation on the consciousness holding boundless space, the consciousness itself becomes our object. Vast, boundaryless consciousness opens in its fullness. This is the opening of consciousness and awareness into the sixth *jhāna*.

To speak of vast, unending consciousness does not make much sense to our conceptual mind and personality. Yet we find universal awareness joined with our awareness, in this vast expanse containing all consciousness. It is as though we have traced a small mountain stream to its source. Its source is a magnificent ocean of knowing consciousness. This knowing quality is not conventional, conceptual knowing. It is direct, experiential, intuitive knowing. It is a kind of knowing wisdom.

Awareness and consciousness are resting in an all-knowing, boundaryless consciousness. It is indescribably magnificent. Awareness can feel and sense the knowing that is contained here. Everything imaginable is referenced here. Recall that the *jhāna* practice is intended to purify the mind. It purifies the mind by inviting awareness out of the small, contained reality of our typical conceptual mind and into a vastness of knowing wisdom that is endless. Our consciousness will never be the same.

It is nearly impossible to communicate the magnitude of abiding in complete union, absorption, with boundless consciousness. This sustained contact forces us to drop the boundaries, the borders, of our particular consciousness, our sense of me. This is an important experience of Awakeness. We awaken from the closely held belief that "I am exclusively this particular body and this familiar consciousness." The Awakeness expands our egoic structures and limitations to a barely perceptible thin layer of individuality.

The Awakeness of abiding in limitless consciousness allows us also to know with certainty that our consciousness is a subset of the Absolute's consciousness. We realize in the experience of Awakeness that we are in an undivided consciousness with the Absolute and all beings simultaneously. Part of the Awakeness of the sixth *jhāna* is deeply knowing that this Absolute consciousness holds and contains the vastness of Absolute space along with boundless space holding all of the form world. We deeply contact and are infused with the expansive, boundaryless reality of Absolute consciousness.

Once we have taken in and released whatever feels outdated and ready to be released in our consciousness while abiding in this *jhāna*, we are ready for the next formless realm—the Base of No-thing-ness, seventh *jhāna*.

Seventh *Jhāna*: The Base of No-thing-ness

As before, we establish awareness and consciousness on the first six *jhānas*. We want to take enough time to feel well seated, well settled, in each *jhāna*. If the energetic field of any particular *jhāna* feels quite strong, that is a sign that more time is needed in that *jhāna*. Once the energy field of each *jhāna* feels well tolerated, then it is time to proceed to the next *jhāna*.

When abiding in the sixth *jhāna*, the second of the formless realms—the Base of Boundless Consciousness—we begin to focus on the absence of the consciousness of space. Recall that space is the fifth *jhāna*, and the absence of the consciousness of boundless space is the seventh *jhāna*.

Remain focusing awareness on the absence of consciousness. That is, the Absence that has the ability and function to hold vast, boundless consciousness. We slowly relax into the vast nothingness. Absolute nothingness, traditionally called "emptiness" in Theravada Buddhism, is unsettling upon first contact. Experiencing the entire universe as absent deeply challenges our framing of identity and our everyday world. We will make repeated journeys into each formless realm, such as the seventh *jhāna*, until its impact, its energetic frequency harmonizes with our perception.

It is a miraculous experience for awareness and consciousness to be resting in the boundless, limitless nothingness holding all of consciousness, which holds all of space. Awareness slowly expands into boundless nothingness. We stretch further and further into vast consciousness, which deeply impacts us, since we do not find a boundary or border. In fact, we do not find anything. Even nothingness is somehow absent from our perception and experience. This nothingness is truly endless and limitless.

The significance of abiding and resting in no-thing-ness cannot be fully communicated. Although no-thing-ness is nothing, it is not simply nothing. It is a bedrock, a foundation, of all reality. No-thing-ness is source emptiness or source Absence. Absence allows us to put down the conceptual knowing and memories we have of our reality. We deeply enter the "don't know" mind of Zen/Chan. When we truly don't know, every minute possibility in the universe is available. This is not a conceptual not knowing. It is a bodily felt "don't know" experience.

The Awakeness of not knowing invites a smooth receptivity, a calm, open assessment of all possibilities. This is a willingness for any result to occur, not just the result we are secretly wishing will happen. We learn to meet reality as it meets itself with complete open acceptance and without preference.

The important impact of Awakeness from sustained abiding in the seventh *jhāna* cannot be overestimated. This is direct, experiential knowing of the nothingness of the Absolute that holds all of consciousness, which holds all space, which holds all form and structure.

In Buddhism we refer to this nothingness as "emptiness." I often use the term "Absence" instead of "emptiness." I feel "Absence" conveys the felt sense of the nothingness of the Absolute most directly and clearly. The nothingness of seventh *jhāna* has a delicate quality to it. It is not just "without." It is "without" with a certain bearing of hereness.

The Awakeness of the nothingness/Absence of the Absolute supports the relaxing and releasing of our concepts and theories about the path, Awakeness, and the realization of a *tathāgata*, a Buddha. This direct Awakeness experience of the vast nothingness of the Absolute helps us soften and release our strictly held concepts of both self and our self's reality. We cannot sustain our self-view as we steep in vast unending nothingness of the Absolute.

When the yogi experiences sustained abiding in the Base of No-thing-ness for an hour or more, then they can orient toward eighth *jhāna*, the Base of Neither Perception nor Non-perception.

Eighth *Jhāna*: The Base of Neither Perception nor Non-perception

We begin by establishing the first through seventh *jhānas*. We want to take sufficient time to feel well grounded, well established in each *jhāna*. As before, should the energetic frequency feel a little intense when abiding in one particular *jhāna*, spend a little more time orienting and energetically harmonizing within that *jhāna*.

After exiting seventh *jhāna* by entering into eighth *jhāna* access concentration, orient toward the awareness that holds the Base of No-thing-ness. Maintain awareness as exclusively as possible on the awareness holding emptiness/ Absence.

The Base of Neither Perception nor Non-perception is principally a direct, pure awareness, that is, awareness without any historical reflections. It is complete present moment awareness. In the Chan/Zen tradition, we refer to direct nonconceptual awareness as "suchness."

In eighth *jhāna*, the fourth formless realm, we abide in nonconceptual reality. We are directly experiencing the Absolute without identity, concept, thought, or intellectual structuring. Nothing is added or explained. This is suchness.

Resting in this formless realm, we see and confirm that reality does not automatically contain concepts or thoughts. We see that we can be merged and absorbed into this non-conceptual, boundaryless vastness with no words, concepts, identity, or historical life reference. This unlocks a deeply known freedom in consciousness. We feel we do not need to know anything to be okay, to be real, to be alive. We also see clearly that our behavior does not hold the meaning we ascribed in our life. We are not the value our actions afford. We truly are the reality abiding in and as the Base of Neither Perception nor Non-perception.

The Awakeness of eighth *jhāna* is incredibly important to the development and realization of the Awakeness of the

Absolute. This formless realm eradicates all concepts, even the concept of no-concept. The Awakeness of the Absolute in this formless realm is so potent we cannot present or sustain any concept, whether of a self or of the everyday world we inhabit. Here, we are without any self or concept of self.

When we have purified the mind sufficiently through resting in eighth *jhāna*, we can orient toward ninth *jhāna*, the Absolute.

Ninth *Jhāna*: Absorption in the Absolute

What I'm referring to as ninth *jhāna* is the direct unity with the Absolute. Some *jhāna* teachers do not include the ninth *jhāna*, but I feel that should a student, a yogi, be able to access the Absolute directly at this stage of the *jhāna* practice, it is incredibly beneficial to welcome that nondual merger with the Absolute.

We begin as we did for eighth *jhāna*, ultimately resting and abiding in first through eighth *jhānas*. Once that energy seems to be well incorporated, the student should rest in the access concentration of eighth *jhāna*, orienting and focusing on the awareness and the Absence and holding the Base of Neither Perception nor Non-perception. By orienting to the awareness and the Absence holding eighth *jhāna*, we begin to make direct contact with the Absolute.

The Absolute is potent with wonderful qualities and functions. One of the most important functions of the Absolute is Absence. In this deep Absence, all phenomena are absorbed into the Absence as the Absolute. Due to this amazing potency, it is advisable to set a time resolve with this *jhāna*.

A time resolve is an express intention to enter and exit a particular *jhāna* at a certain time. For example, we could set the time resolve "May first *jhāna* arise for sixty minutes." If our meditative concentration, our unifying, purifying mind, is sufficiently agile, awareness will enter and exit the *jhāna* close to the time resolve intended.

The Awakeness of ninth *jhāna*—the Absolute realm—cannot be fully stated. It is nonconceptual direct intuitive knowing. We perceive by knowing contact rather than reflective association.

In this realm, there is no identity, no location, no time, no concept, no thought. Yet there is a fullness, a knowing that penetrates through all identity and conceptual understanding. The Absolute realm is the base, the potent force, of all Awakeness.

In this Awakeness we learn to deeply surrender all phenomena, any understanding, any practices, any attainments, any memories, any identities. We must surrender everything we normally hold close. This Awakeness requires a complete letting go. Even letting go and surrender must be surrendered and let go.

After steeping in this realm for sixty minutes without interruption, we can orient toward the source of the Absolute: Cessation.

CESSATION

CESSATION IS PROBABLY the most important topic Buddhists should be endeavoring to thoroughly understand. Cessation is the origin of all reality. It is our origin as well. It is the center, the source of the Absolute.

I will share my experience with Cessation in an attempt to describe the indescribable.

I first encountered Cessation during the two-month retreat I completed with my Theravada Buddhist meditation master. Until that retreat, I do not believe I had even heard of Cessation in my then thirty years of Zen practice.

After completing extensive work using all ten *kasinas* for three hours each in eighth *jhāna*, my awareness was both deeply concentrated and unified, with a startling ability to penetrate any object or reality awareness touched.

While resting in the eighth *jhāna* access concentration, I oriented awareness toward the Absence/emptiness, particularly toward profound peace and majestic stillness. As consciousness and awareness began to harmonize with

the profound peace and majestic stillness, the Absence/
emptiness of the Absolute realm began to be revealed. This
was not simply an experience; it was complete merging
into and with the Absolute. No sense of a me or thoughts
could exist here. There was no location of perception. Pure
awareness unfolded. The Beingness of the Absolute along
with an encompassing love subsumed whatever was left of
a subjective awareness. The viewpoint was of and from the
Absolute itself.

Deepening in the Absolute, without a here or there, was
a vastness beyond imagination. Awareness opened in each
direction, in a directionless realm, confirming that there
were no boundaries. No border or edges. It was indeed truly
boundless. Rather than that confirmation creating any reactivity, the experience was of deep comfort. The Absolute was
experientially real.

Perception of wise knowing embraced peace, stillness,
emptiness, pure love, pure awareness, and pure Presence. My
resting awareness in these pure, undifferentiated qualities
and interwoven functions landed deeply and well in consciousness. There was no distinction between consciousness
and the many potent functions of the Absolute.

Awareness settled on peace, stillness, and Absence. These
continued deepening without changing at all. There was deepening without a start or finish. It simply was. Journeying in the
Absolute was also a matter of effortlessly inclining awareness.
There would be a seeming spot in the distance. Awareness

would connect with that spot. Awareness would immediately be at the spot. It was both distant and near simultaneously. This is a confounding concept to try to unpack later with thought. In the Absolute, reality is both here and there. There is no time, distance, or space.

As awareness continued deepening in the peace, stillness, and Absence, a deepening quiet enveloped awareness. Any potential to reflect through direct experience of the Absolute slowed to a stop.

Peace and stillness continued to quiet all activity including no activity. In other words, as reflection quieted every mental polarity, such as knowing or not knowing and perception or non-perception, effort and effortlessness quietly ceased.

Sensing that Cessation was imminent through its engaged pull, I set a time resolve to enter and abide in and as Cessation for three hours.

The non-presence of Cessation began to experientially appear. It felt like an enormous void of peace, stillness, and emptiness welcoming, embracing, subsuming all of reality. All form and formlessness began and concluded here. This was the source of the Absolute.

Cessation snagged awareness. Awareness willingly became enmeshed with Absence, opening to Cessation. In the commencement of Cessation, all mental activity of any kind ceased. All materiality, all forms of physicality, even the structure of thought and identity, ceased. There was a vast, void darkness that cannot be labeled as darkness. Deep peace enveloped. There was no mental or material activity, effort, or reflection. There was nothing. It was a "lights out" experience. There was the most potent nothingness imaginable.

A startling Awakeness snapped me to awareness after three hours. Tears fell as I wept deeply. The Source of all reality was appearing and functioning as me. The beauty, the generosity, the simple sophistication of the Absolute and Cessation began to slowly land.

This experience of Awakeness far overshadowed any *kenshō*, *kōan*, or *jhāna* experience. It was both primary and the most sophisticated experience possible. It was not an experience I had; it was the Absolute's experience of itself, its core, as Cessation that happened in my unknown location.

Because Cessation arose for such a significant period of time, I was seriously blown out of any and all reality I held or had held. It took me around eighteen months to integrate most of this experience. Then, I needed a few years to deepen, mature, and embody this fundamentally potent reality. Since that experience in 2005, I have continued to open to Cessation, including teaching its practice through my guided journeys into the Absolute and to the portal of Cessation.

After that deep, sustained experience of Cessation, I was left with the potent Awakeness of Cessation. Through the surrender of all identity and concepts, I was able to rest, abide even, in the origin of Awakeness itself.

Cessation allows us to turn all our energies and mental activity off. Even in sleep and dreaming, we have some concepts and identity operating. In Cessation and its Awakeness, we have a deep stillness, a peace that smooths out all the wrinkles of an egoic structure. It is not that these qualities disappear forever. Rather, they are seen thoroughly when present and profoundly known to be expressions from Cessation.

All activity arises and returns to Cessation. It is the primary Awakeness upon which all other expressions and experiences of Awakening originate.

PRACTICES AFTER CESSATION AWAKENING

ONCE WE HAVE steeped in the completeness of Cessation, it is valuable to understand how we are structured and oriented as humans. This means to also deeply understand the Buddhist path and its journeys of spiritual practice.

After the Buddha experienced the Great Awakening, he spent some time pondering its impact and reflecting on what he should do next. He wondered if the world was capable of understanding the truth of which he was an expression. Ultimately, he decided to seek out the fellow sadhus, wandering mystics, with whom he had previously practiced. He felt they had "little dust in their eyes" and could potentially receive the teaching and practices he was offering.

The Buddha taught these sadhus the Four Noble Truths: Human life is suffering (*dukkha*), the origin of this suffering is craving (*samudaya*), the ceasing of this suffering is Cessation (*nirodha*), and the path to liberation (*marga*) is called the Eightfold Path.

Accordingly, after my experience of Cessation, I found myself returning to an in-depth study of the Four Noble Truths and the Eightfold Path.

After Awakening, applying the Four Noble Truths and Eightfold Path allows the practitioner to expressly, consciously engage their life to more fully understand human suffering while expressing Awakeness and maintaining an openness to further experiences of Awakening. Each experience of Awakening deepens the quality and function of Awakeness.

The Four Noble Truths

The Four Noble Truths are axiomatic truths of humanity. Being in human existence—that is, conditioned reality— means that everything in this reality will one day decay and die. Nothing that is conditioned lasts forever. This truth in itself contains suffering. The only potential to concurrently rest in what is not conditioned—that is, what does not decay and die, the Absolute—is through the practice and experience of Awakening and its resulting Awakeness.

The Four Noble Truths are *dukkha*, *samudaya*, *nirodha*, and *marga*.

Dukkha (Dissatisfactoriness and Suffering)

Dukkha is chronic dissatisfactoriness. It appears when we

- get what we want but it ends too early,
- do not get what we want,

— try to get away from what we really do not want, and

— are confused about what to want and what to reject.

These responses have one thing in common: They are conditioned, that is, from the world of cause and effect. These are also referred to as temporary.

In Buddhism, we talk about a "second arrow." The first arrow is the event that opens to suffering. The second arrow is the judgment, blame, and negative self-talk that swiftly accompanies the first arrow of direct experience. The addition of the second arrow of judgment is what contributes to and exacerbates our mental suffering, or *dukkha*. For most people, the second arrow is the most difficult part of suffering. These ruminating judgments and self-blame plague most people throughout their lives.

Samudaya (Origin of Suffering)

When our longing ache for possessions and relationships couples with our *dukkha*, a deep-seated craving is the result. That craving, *samudaya*, is the overwhelming inner wanting of something or someone to relieve us of our aching discomfort and lifelong feelings of worthlessness.

A significant portion of *samudaya* is rooted in our belief in the me. When we firmly believe in the self, we are typically in direct contact with the craving, misunderstandings, and demands of the self. It wants unwavering support and constant feeding with affirmations and victories in life.

These affirmations and successes prove to our self and the world that we are a person of significance.

Nirodha (Cessation of Suffering)

Nirodha is another word for Cessation. The experience of Cessation is the only direct experience that can significantly and substantially uproot the firm belief in the self as an enduring entity. In Cessation, awareness is merged in deep peace, stillness, silence, and Absence/emptiness. Should this be a sustained experience to activate profound Awakeness, the structures of the self are significantly weakened.

Following the direct experience of Cessation, we clearly know what is conditioned in our life and what is the truest unconditioned reality of the Absolute. The Absence quality of the Absolute realm reveals that which is unconditioned (that is, without cause), unborn, uncreated. Absence plays a pivotal role in our spiritual path by repeatedly weakening the belief in the psychological structure called me. As our sense of self softens in meeting the Absolute, we begin to relax our belief that the self and the world of temporary pleasure are the most real. The world of pleasure, our everyday world, begins to hold less and less pull. Our compulsions to exclusively seek pleasure relax. We can be content.

Marga (Path to Cessation)

The path or *marga* in Buddhism is what we call the Eightfold Path. Through developing and cultivating the eight properties of the path, we come to see with the eye of unity, the eye of the unborn, the wisdom eye. By repeatedly witnessing that which is uncreated and unconditioned, as well as what is created, we more deeply witness and experience reality as it is.

It is expected that all Buddhists will develop and cultivate each of the components of the Eightfold Path.

The Eightfold Path

The Buddha outlined and taught an engaging life practice we call the Eightfold Path. Buddhists the world over develop their contact with and expression of each of the path's eight components: right view, right resolve, right speech, right action, right livelihood, right effort, right awareness, and right samadhi.

It is a never-ending, ever-deepening practice path, as we discover profound meaning the further we walk it.

Right view: viewing from the truth of *dukkha* (dissatisfactoriness and suffering) and from the experience of *nirodha* of the unborn, unconditioned. Right view means we are looking from the truth of the Absolute as our source and from Cessation as the hub, the core of the Absolute. We increasingly witness customary reality concurrently with the extraordinary reality of the Absolute manifesting as all created life forms, formlessness, and beings.

Right resolve: resolving to turn toward ultimate truth and live from our depth of clear understanding and Awakening. Right resolve holds dear the intention to orient toward the truth of the Absolute and its core Cessation as the deepest purest reality. Yet as humans, we function in a conditioned world of cause and effect. We increasingly learn to hold each of these views as these worlds intertwine.

Right speech: using speech that is unifying, not divisive; saying what is true; avoiding gossip and idle/unnecessary speech. Right speech is committing to speaking truth as often and fully as is possible. Because we must maintain sensitivity to what others can hear or experience, we will need to adjust our speech based upon the emotional maturity, understanding of truth, and spiritual experience of the listener.

Right action: acting from our clear knowing, from the lack of an abiding self, from nondual unity, from clarity and love. Right action is taking action that is most beneficial to all beings while holding sufficient sensitivity to the perception of those around us. Right action is typically the most wholesome, inclusive action available in a particular moment.

Right livelihood: engaging in work that promotes unity, clarity of understanding, and honors all life as an expression of the indivisible unity of the Absolute realm, our source. Right livelihood is offering ourselves in service to our deepest truth while causing as little harm to ourselves and to all beings everywhere.

Right effort: using clarity-of-being energy rather than doing energy. Clarity-of-being energy is unconditioned and has no birth and no death; activity spontaneously arises. Right effort is taking action with the deepest grounding in truth we can hold. It is trying to act out of the generosity and inclusion of the Absolute rather than from a selfish motivation.

Right awareness: maintaining a viewpoint from our deepest experienced truth rather than the conventional dualistic mind. It is a willingness to perceive and be aware from the unified, unconditioned mind. Right awareness is intending to do good for as many other beings as possible in each action we take.

Right samadhi: developing and using concentration meditation (that is, breath awareness, *kasinas*, or heart practices) to sharpen and focus awareness to penetrate conventional perspectives and see what is objective, universal, unconditioned truth. Right samadhi means to develop our concentration meditation as deeply as is possible. We should seek out experts in concentration meditation with whom to study. We should be diligent in learning the meditations and practices that deepen and sustain concentration meditation.

SAMADHI AWAKENING PRACTICES

CONCENTRATION MEDITATION practices, called samadhi, help us by increasingly focusing our awareness into the deepest meditative concentration available to us.

Deep, focused meditative awareness will allow us to penetrate and clarify the Absolute heart qualities in our heart's consciousness. As we continue deepening our meditative concentration, we can then turn this penetrating concentration toward the heart issues we each carry. In Buddhism, we do this through the heart meditations and practices, called the *brahmavihāras*.

In the process of contacting and deeply resting in these heart qualities of the Absolute, we begin to replace our emotional and psychologically based heart qualities. In other words, we begin to replace our temporal emotions with Absolute heart qualities. These Absolute heart qualities are not conditioned by our wants and cravings. Rather these heart qualities arise spontaneously without the effort of a me. The *brahmavihāras* are a samadhi practice that focuses deeply on the Absolute heart qualities and expressions of love. Other samadhi practices cultivate an "absence of self"—what is traditionally called "no-self"—experience.

The *Brahmavihāras*: Heart-opening Awakeness

The *brahmavihāras* provide an important practice vehicle for Awakening and unity experiences. "*Brahmavihāras*" is most commonly translated as "divine abodes," sacred expressions in which we can abide or deeply root and rest. These are the ancient unconditioned heart practices of traditional Theravada Buddhism.

As with anything that is of the source—the Absolute— each heart quality is by nature unconditioned. This means we do not need to make, produce, generate, or direct the heart quality itself. It is already in consciousness awaiting our discovery of its existence. Additionally, these unconditioned heart qualities will not fade or become unavailable should we make errors or mistakes in life. The Absolute is incapable of being punitive in response to our mistaken beliefs or actions.

The Awakeness of the *brahmavihāras* is always heart based. Practicing the *brahmavihāras*, particularly on deep retreat, softens our resistance to experiencing these heart qualities. Our resistance usually comes from our secret feelings of unworthiness.

To fully experience the depths and benefits of the heart meditations and practices, we must be willing to risk all patterns of mind and personality-driven behaviors. Any perception of separation between our awareness of our heart and the Absolute heart must be welcomed for exploration. We need to be willing to test our beliefs in how our heart and emotions function to reveal the deepest truth available to each of us. In engaging in these pivotal, life-changing meditation practices, we must be rigorously honest with ourselves. Each *brahmavihāra* serves a different function of purification and expression of the Absolute love.

The four divine abodes are *upekkhā* (equanimity), *karunā* (compassion), *mudita* (empathetic joy), and *mettā* (unconditioned, unborn love). Each *brahmavihāra* has its own world of qualities and applications.

Upekkhā (Equanimity)

Upekkhā is about deep, unreserved acceptance of truth. It is not trying to assert our personal truth or what we desire to be the truth. It is unreservedly aligning with the truth that is actually present. We do this by simply silently repeating the word "acceptance" when we encounter a situation in which we feel unsettled. If we wish to alter or change the moment in any way, we are resisting this very moment of experience.

Upekkhā's Awakeness teaches us the objective love, the profound acceptance of the Absolute. The Absolute is not personal and relates to all other beings objectively with complete love. This means we are each as fully loved and accepted as every other being. The Absolute's objective love helps us soften our allegiance to maintaining our personal stories about our life's pain and suffering. This pain and suffering is the foundation that supports our sense of self.

Karunā (Compassion)

Karunā is about being intimate with our discomfort, dissatisfactoriness, or painful suffering. *Karunā* helps us learn to be more fully open and present to what is uncomfortable in life. All beings attempt to avoid what is not desired and seek what is most desired. Yet our life experience teaches us repeatedly that life is disappointing. Every day, we are unable to receive everything we desire. Additionally, life contains events that result in injury or loss. We cannot avoid life's losses. Yet we can learn to hold them with increasing tenderness and love.

By opening unreservedly to the fullness of our discomfort or pain, we remove or reduce the judgments opposing the suffering. Because many of us identify with life losses, they remain subjective. Subjective losses mean the loss is mine, is part of my self-definition.

By repeatedly returning to being with our losses as fully as possible, we invite the tender love of the Absolute's compassion. This tender love allows us to begin shifting our way of seeing. Instead of identifying with life losses, making them a part of who are, we shift to seeing the losses as independent of ourselves. Life losses are not who we are but rather what has happened to us. When we can witness life losses as objective, what happens to me rather than *as* me, we can engage and work with them.

Karunā's Awakeness is opening to the pain and suffering endemic to our life. It is opening to the pain and discomfort we experience without creating stories of righteous victimhood or anger directed at those identified as the sources of suffering. The Awakeness here is supple. It opens and meets, helps to hold, whatever pain or suffering arises. It relaxes any stories associated with the pain. It allows our awareness to drop beneath our stories of me and meet the discomfort directly with full and tender acceptance.

Mudītā (Empathetic Love)

Mudita is the undivided Oneness of love that includes all without qualification. From the inherent Oneness of the Absolute, we authentically and literally experience another's happiness, success, or joy as our own. *Mudītā* softens barriers we uphold between you and me.

Typically, humans wish to maintain set boundaries between ourselves and others. We safeguard our pain to maintain an inner identity of a wounded soul. By maintaining the inner core wound, we excuse ourselves from taking full responsibility for our attitudes and behaviors. It is counterintuitive that we would elect to maintain this perception of inner wounding. Because it is intertwined with our sense of self, we protect it.

Mudita's Awakeness is one of concerned care and supportive love of the Absolute. It gently dissolves the boundaries or borders we establish that separate us from our world. This openhanded, generous spirit cultivates an undivided Oneness of complete, perfect love. In love there is only a willingness to share resources. It would be unimaginable to hoard preciousness from others.

Mettā (Unborn, Unconditioned Love)

With the unborn, unconditioned, uncreated love of *mettā*, we soften and release any and all inner beliefs about our restrictions or limitations to truly, unreservedly support another. We do not create or direct this conditioned, unborn love. We simply rest in it until it begins to overflow from our personal consciousness. As *mettā* overflows, we can gently hold whichever dear one to whom we are willing to offer loving support. *Mettā* will find its heart-home in the other dear soul we wish to receive the Absolute's love.

In my experience and teaching, *mettā* is the source, the origin, of all the applications and functions of each quality or function of the Absolute's love. It is an unrestrained, unreserved love available to all beings equally and fully.

No-self Awakeness

Concentration meditation is where the focus, the object, of the meditative awareness is unchanging. We derive benefit from taking up and holding tenderly a single meditative object. We focus concentrating awareness in one direction or location, choosing to prioritize that single meditative object over all else in experience and perception.

In meditative concentration, we withdraw our mental energy, our awareness, from the many mundane mind attractions, including reinforcing the sense of self through near constant attention and fascination. In effect, we are freeing the mind by repeatedly electing to rest awareness on the one meditative object rather than all the mental distractions we are accustomed to meeting. This is deeply relaxing and liberating. It is a relief to redirect mental awareness to a single meditative object instead of the typical past memories or future planning projects. We can more fully rest in this present moment, the moment of now.

Additionally, resting awareness with our meditative object invites deepening meditative concentration. In effect, we are resting in the wonderful qualities of the Absolute, such as peace, stillness, Presence, and love.

In my teaching, I emphasize dropping beneath the conceptual level of contact to a nonconceptual direct experience of the meditative object. We can recognize we are meditating at a conceptual level when we are making mental associations with the meditative object, remembering facts about the meditative object, or in any other way mentally reflecting on the object. We can see we are creating and maintaining a separation between present moment awareness and our meditative object. Learning to meditatively concentrate allows us to reveal nonconceptual reality within our own experience.

As an example, in my book *Liberating the Self* I write about the meditation practice "Thirty-Two Body Parts." This is a meditation where we systematically engage different body parts, such as head hair, body hair, and skin. We make first contact with the conceptual understanding of each part. Taking my hair as a meditative object, I will typically first encounter my opinion, memories, and judgments about head hair. I may remember having bad haircuts or regret a hairstyle choice from the past.

As our meditative concentration deepens, we begin to drop beneath the story, the memory, the concept of head hair and make direct nonconceptual contact with head hair. We begin to experience head hair directly without any conceptual overlay.

In such a direct, nonconceptual contact with head hair, we come to land on what head hair means outside the history and story we hold of our head hair. Interestingly, we each have a certain history and invested identity with our body parts. Steeping meditatively beneath the body parts' concepts, we loosen and open our self-definition to include greater nonconceptual reality. This loosens our allegiance to our sense of self and our story of me and helps us cultivate our no-self experience.

This cultivated disidentification with our body parts as identity of self is freeing. We encounter unfamiliar viewpoints and realities. This returns us to the vast openness of wonder at the mystery that is the Absolute in all its fascinating expressions of life.

The Zen Path of Awakeness

After a satori-level Awakening, true nature shifts to become the foundation of identity. Concepts are then useful to explain ideas but have no greater value than a calculator resting on your desk.

BUDDHISM HAS ALWAYS embraced, respected, and incorporated the indigenous practices of each country to which it was introduced. When Buddhism migrated from India to China, a shift took place; Buddhism incorporated some of the understandings of both Confucianism and Taoism into a new understanding of Buddhism.

Confucianism provided a deep respect, a reverence, for the lineage, the history of the practice family to which we each belong. Taoism rooted Buddhism in developing the subtle energy in the body, mind, and universe. This modified Buddhism became known as "Chana," the Chinese pronunciation of the deep meditative concentration states of Theravada Buddhism called *jhāna*. "Chana" was later shortened to "Chan," pronounced "Zen" in Japanese and "Son" in Korean.

A few of the practices of this new adaptation of Buddhism are the Three Great Vows, *shikantaza* (just sitting), and *kōan* study. These Zen practices can support a sudden, direct Awakening called *kenshō*. *Kenshō* and Cessation are both Awakening experiences. Both afford us direct contact with the Absolute. An Awakening experience is a direct experience of the Absolute realizing itself in the location of a particular consciousness. The lingering aftereffect of an Awakening experience is the flowering of Awakeness.

The Three Great Vows are the foundation upon which *shikantaza* and *kōan* study can find a home and become a catalyst for Awakening. When we orient toward and land in the Three Great Vows, they build and shape our bearings and position. They inform our approach to the Zen path of practice and to the fruit of either *kenshō* or Cessation experiences. The Three Great Vows are penetrating truths. We will engage with each vow being drawn deeper into the Absolute.

In *shikantaza* we are opening to the Awakeness of the Absolute directly. We are trying to release our attachments and identities in a wholesome manner. We are not trying to reject or remove attachments and identities. We are simply preferencing these vehicles of Awakening over our custom-ary manner of thought and concept. The result of engaging *shikantaza* allows us to silently steep in the potency of the Absolute. We are reorienting our inner compass toward the Absolute from our customary life. In time, the seat of iden-tity shifts from the me to the Absolute through the process of Awakening.

In formal *kōan* study, we are using nonconceptual stories of dharma exchanges between roshis and students that cut through identity and conceptual beliefs. By taking up each *kōan* and consuming it entirely, we become the *kōan*.

The *kōans* are confounding to our customary thinking process. When we first take up a *kōan*, we try to figure it out as we would solve any life problem. When we start receiving a rejection of our conceptual answers, we grow frustrated. We begin to realize our usual way of problem-solving is not working. Only once we give up our usual way of thinking and problem-solving do we start to engage the *kōan* with our intuitive knowing and intuitive wisdom. We learn to hold the *kōan* day and night. Eventually, when we are keeping it on the "tip of our breath," we can begin to more deeply penetrate the experiential truth of the *kōan*.

A further technique in *kōan* study is to enter and abide in each person's consciousness within the *kōan*. By directly engaging the consciousness of each *kōan* participant, we can see the stickiness of the student and the freedom of the roshi. Typically, we identify mostly with the student and scratch our heads when reflecting on the roshi's unexpected behavior and puzzling actions. Witnessing this behavior loosens our investment in a story of the *kōan* and opens us to other realities.

—

THREE GREAT VOWS

FROM THE BUDDHA'S never-ending Awakening and the teaching emanating from the resulting Awakeness, the Chan/Zen tradition developed the Three Great Vows: Great Faith, Great Determination, and Great Doubt. These vows provide a framework for our spiritual practice. In addition, the Three Great Vows are each an important portal for accessing the Absolute directly.

Great Faith

Normally when we use the word "faith," we mean a belief in something we cannot fully know or confirm for ourselves. In effect we take some information, some reality, as real.

In the Zen tradition, it is axiomatic that all beings are imbued with Buddha nature. Buddha nature is the Presence and functioning of the Absolute in our individual consciousness and life. It is the real potential for each sentient being to be a fully awake and functioning expression of the Absolute.

If the full Awakeness of the Absolute were something remote and distant from us, we would have to find ways to go and get it or have someone with greater experience or skill offer it to us. No legitimate spiritual teacher claims to have the power to act fully as a substitute for the Absolute; we are each nothing but the Absolute. Yet Awakeness of the Absolute must be preceded by a recognized experience of the Absolute Awakening to itself. This is the most teachers can offer: to be a conduit, a catalyst of the Absolute, hopefully triggering Awakening. Some teachers can spark Awakening as the Absolute ignites the fuse of Awakening in students.

Students who have yet to have a confirmed Awakening experience must initially take the potential of Awakening on faith, trusting in the texts and teachers until they can experientially confirm it. Teachers confirm Awakening experiences through their prior experience of Awakening as well as through their growing familiarity of the Absolute's functioning. This is a kind of quality control in the Zen tradition.

Similarly, the Zen texts confirm the inherent ability and functioning of Awakening in each sentient being. This is communicated in *kōan* study as well as in sutras, the Buddha's sermons, and other sacred texts. This information cumulatively affords the student the opportunity to base their faith on the history of Zen as lived by their teacher.

Great Faith Exercise

- While meditating quietly, gently invite the question "Is Awakening real?"

- Notice your first reaction or response. Many people feel that the possibility of Awakening is real for almost everyone except themselves. Students typically make contact with the inner sense of worthlessness when holding the question of Awakening. They feel their perceived lifetime story of brokenness and worthlessness permanently excludes them from deep realization of the Absolute in Awakening.

- Open to any hesitation or reluctance to accept the fact, the reality, of your Buddha nature. Allow an image of your closest teacher to abide in awareness. Include all teachers who you feel are deeply awake. Recall the Awakening stories you have heard or read. Ask yourself, Do I believe these Awakening stories?

- When you answer "yes" to the belief in Awakening stories, let the truth of Awakening take hold in your consciousness. Feel your confidence expand due to the potential of Awakening for all sentient beings.

— As this confidence, this "yes," grows while deepening its roots, feel the certainty in your *hara*
as it's called in the Zen tradition—your belly's
energetic center or chakra. The *hara* is located
about two fingerbreadths below the navel and
two to three fingerbreadths in from the surface
of the skin. The *hara* allows awareness to rest
in a settled, fairly nonconceptual energy center.
Some students report perceiving a vastness,
an open void, while resting in the *hara*. Each
energy center or chakra can directly open to the
Absolute.

— You may find it supportive to place your right
hand over your *hara*. Breathe into the *hara* if possible as you feel your confidence in Awakening
increasing.

Great Determination

Typically, when we speak of determination or effort, we are referring to an act of doing of the egoic personality, where one's self is taking a certain action to produce a specific result. This is not the kind of determination I am referencing here. The determination I am referring to here is the effortless, no-self direction from our true nature, the Absolute in our particular consciousness. This begins with an intention, an aspiration, a wish, to deepen our connection with the Absolute.

Many people beginning a spiritual or meditative path have already had one or more dramatic transcendent experiences of union or deep contact with the source, the Absolute. They are drawn to return and increase, or repeat, this experience of connection.

We are mostly rooted in our egoic wanting, the desire of the personality. This personality structuring seeks deeper connection with our true nature and the Absolute from a possessive viewpoint. We want to accumulate contact and make it our possession. Predictably, this does not work. Our personal egoic effort can only reach so far toward deeper connection with the Absolute. At some point, the personality's reach for connection fails. It fails because it is not being pursued for the benefit of all beings but rather for the singular benefit to our sense of self, the me. We will often see signs of limitation because we are pursuing a spiritual goal for the sake of the me.

As we each begin to orient toward our source—the Absolute—our efforts, our determinations, begin to change to a more wholesome orientation. When our motivation shifts to resting in and expressing the Absolute, it shifts to a more altruistic grounding. We are intending actions that more and more are geared to benefit all beings, rather than just ourselves personally.

In addition, we each have an inner drive, an enlightenment drive, called *bodhicitta* in Buddhism, toward complete union with the Absolute. We hunger to release our allegiance to our personality patterns and embrace the wholesome freedom of the Absolute. This inner drive for communion and merging with the Absolute becomes our deepest, sincerest motivation—our great determination.

Great Determination Exercise

- When deeply settled into your meditation, sense into the *hara*, your belly center or chakra.

- Resting there, feel the call of the Absolute. Sense into the desire, the attraction, to return to full union with the Absolute. This is our *bodhicitta*, our drive or wholesome desire for Awakening and living a life of Awakeness.

- Open to your drive for enlightenment. This is a drive that benefits all beings, not just ourselves.

- Feel the solidity of the *hara*. Sense the quiet confidence in the *hara*. Let that quiet confidence open and expand as fully as it wishes in consciousness.

Great Doubt

For most of us, when we deeply "know" something, we hold it close. We then begin to defend our conclusions based on that particular knowing. This is one of the ways people become more fixed, unmoving, and inflexible. As you can imagine, this leaves little room for new information or new "knowings."

Great Doubt points to the mysterious nature of the Absolute. Regardless of our level of intense commitment to our spiritual practice path, we continue the human pattern of holding dear what we feel we know with unshakable confidence. Unfortunately, being more fixed in our beliefs, concepts, and opinions about our spiritual path begins to block what we do not yet know through direct experience. In effect, we leave less and less openness in our consciousness to explore the great mystery that is the Absolute.

Great Doubt is a reminder to hold loosely, lightly even, whatever conclusions we have reached or plateaus of Awakening we have beheld breathlessly. By staying soft with our knowings, we leave room for new information to enter.

Earlier in this lifetime I worked as a lawyer, a litigation attorney. One of the most important lessons I learned in this role was to revisit any opinion or conclusions previously reached whenever new information, new facts, and new experiences arose. In other words, I put aside my prior conclusions or beliefs about a person or the direction of a litigation case when factoring in the new information. This allowed me to fully integrate important new information or unexpected experiences and potentially reach a new conclusion.

In this way, you give new experience and new knowings the space, the openness, to land as potently as possible. Maintaining contact with Great Doubt allows us to rest in true humility with openness and respect.

Great Doubt Exercise

- Settle into your customary meditation.

- Once well settled, let awareness open to what you do not know.

- One way to contact Great Doubt is to imagine yourself facing a whiteboard with the most complex math problem you have ever seen. It is so complex you have no chance or possibility of deciphering it. Another approach is to imagine you are in a foreign country where you do not speak or understand the language. It should be a language you cannot figure out.

- Feel the problem and your inability to solve it easily. Sense the reality that you do not have any idea how to solve the math problem or understand the foreign language. You legitimately do not know this answer.

- Rest in not knowing, the unknown. Whatever is unknown to us contains every possibility for resolution.

- Notice any feelings of discomfort in not knowing. Is it possible to accept and hold your not knowing and your inability to solve these problems without resistance?

SHIKANTAZA

SHIKANTAZA—silent illumination meditation—is taught primarily in the Zen lineages. It is often translated from the Japanese as "just sitting." Practicing *shikantaza* is resting in and as Awakeness itself.

Shikantaza is intended to slowly break down your identity and allegiance to this body and mind as being me. The Awakeness here softens our beliefs about who we are and how the world operates. This Awakeness supports "not knowing." In not knowing, every possibility is available. Once we begin to know something, we limit the possible choices, conclusions, or experiences.

The Awakeness of *shikantaza* invites the Presence, the radiance, of the Absolute into our consciousness as it expresses its Awakeness through our direct lived experience. In *shikantaza*, we open to and rest deeply in the Absolute itself. We steep in its mystery and in the vast nothingness of the Absolute.

When we begin silent illumination meditation, we start with awareness revealing the unity inherent in our entire body and mind. The body and mind settle into an undivided Oneness of experienced flow of awareness. The felt sense of the body and mind merging is a quality of inner flow. When we experience inner flow, awareness is not conceptually divided into head versus nonhead, or body. The inner flow is a unified body/mind.

Yet we conceptually hold our body and mind as two separate parts. In this meditation, by being with both the body and mind simultaneously without doing anything, the conceptual divisions soften and drop. We experience and rest in a unified wholeness within.

As we settle further into *shikantaza*, perception of inner and outer atmospheres relax into a Oneness of awareness. The felt sense is that there is a soft distinction between inner and outer worlds. We experience the division between inner and outer as a primary self-identity of the body boundary. The body boundary is the outer perception of this body. Simply put, it is where "I" cease in my own perception. Here, too, the conceptual divide between inner and outer awareness and experience softens into a unified, flowing Oneness with no discernible inside or outside. There is a sense of flowing and cohesion of inner and outer.

After further settling into *shikantaza*, the Oneness of merged inner and outer awareness expands and extends into a nothingness, a vastness without boundary, border, or limit of any kind. Truly, awareness does not actually expand. Instead, our limiting concepts of spaciousness soften and drop through being with awareness, without any intention or doing. We realize awareness is never divided into mine or yours. It simply is.

Awareness is a vast, open, inclusive spaciousness of pure perception without qualitative limit or end. Our conceptual definition of body, mind, inner, outer, far, and near soften into a unified field of a profound vast Oneness of experienced awareness.

When I learned *shikantaza* about fifty years ago, great attention and instruction was offered relating to body posture, placement of robes, etc. There were no instructions on what to do in the meditation. When I approached and asked those more senior to me what they were doing in *shikantaza*, each person gave me a different answer. I concluded there was no technique or progression for the meditation.

I have sometimes referred to my experience of early Zen meditation as like being a hot-air balloon pilot. I could get the balloon in the air but never knew which way it would travel or where it would land. In other words, I had no inner meditative practice or technique. It was always a random experience of meditation.

As I teach *shikantaza*, I include the three stages elucidated by the Chan teachers:

1 Unity of body and mind
2 Unity of inner and outer atmospheres
3 Opening to the vastness or void

Shikantaza Practice

- Seat yourself in a comfortable position, and place your hands in your lap or high on your thighs.

- Take a few deep centering belly breaths, inhaling and exhaling as thoroughly as possible.

- Feel your contact with the ground while including the supported safety of the floor and the building you are in. See if you can feel the support of the earth beneath you holding each of us right in this moment.

- With eyes closed halfway and with a soft gaze, make contact with the *hara*. It can be either a visual perception or a felt-sense perception. It does not matter which is present. Should you be accustomed to meditating with your eyes closed, that is fine too.

- Rest your awareness in and on the energetic felt sense in the *hara*. You may feel a spacious grounding, an expansive vast blackness. Do not do anything. Just be with the flow of radiant spaciousness in this very moment.

- Maintain alert perception.

— Breathe and be the radiant spaciousness that you are and have always been.

— When you feel well settled in the *hara*, invite awareness to the heart center or chakra. This is not the human heart but the chest cavity itself.

— As you breathe into the heart chakra, sense around the edges of awareness. Often the Absolute's heart qualities and functions are subtle and can be located around the edges of awareness.

— Let the radiance of the Absolute's heart qualities of unborn love, deep compassion, loving empathetic joy, and deep acceptance steep in your consciousness.

— On the next in-breath, invite awareness to the center of the forehead—the wisdom or dharma eye. The wisdom eye is an essential tool or skill to cultivate. The wisdom or dharma eye supports us in developing inner meditative sight. In effect, some people can see their meditation object and the development of the meditation. Others do not see with the wisdom eye but rather cultivate the felt sense of meditation. They can feel the underlying tone and existence of the meditation object or practice. For both these groups, developing contact with the wisdom eye is essential.

— When you feel well settled in the wisdom eye, invite awareness to the top of the head. This is the crown chakra. The crown chakra is an important energy center for spiritual practice, particularly meditation and prayer. When distant formless realms open to our awareness and consciousness, these exit the body through the crown chakra. Additionally, we can receive "knowing downloads" from the Absolute at appropriate times.

— When you feel well established in the crown chakra, let awareness touch an area about eighteen inches or half a meter above the crown chakra. I call this the universal chakra. This chakra has an extremely objective, neutral energetic feel to it. Rest awareness in the universal chakra.

— Resting easefully in the universal chakra, turn awareness to your interiority, the inner body. Ask the direct question, Are mind and body unified or not? Should you perceive mind and body in a unity, a Oneness, rest in that Oneness. On the other hand, should you feel mind in your head area and body from the neck down, that suggests a division between mind and body. Hold the head as mind, the rest of the body as body, including the perception of separation of these two. Hold all as one. The division between mind and body is purely conceptual. Maintaining awareness on mind, body, and separation allows and invites the unconditioned to meet the conditioned separation. The conceptual separation of mind and body cannot be sustained in direct contact with the unconditioned, the Absolute. The separation will fall away in time.

— Once the body and mind are flowing in a perceptual unity, rest in the unity as interior atmosphere. Taking body-mind unity as your interior atmosphere, invite awareness to contact the outer atmosphere—the space outside the body boundary or body's edge. Are the inner and outer atmosphere the same or different? If the inner and outer atmosphere feel identical, rest in the sameness of this energy, including the body boundary in your perception and experience. The body boundary, that is, the skin, is one of our most primary identities. It was established as a me before we had language skills. Thus, it is a preverbal identity.

— As inner and outer atmosphere begin to harmonize—that is, find a matching energetic tone—we will witness the body boundary begin to dissolve. The body's location may also shift dramatically. It's possible to feel that the left arm is two meters

in that direction and the right leg is a meter in
the opposite direction. We can even perceive that
our head is missing. We literally cannot sense the
head's physicality in this experience.

— When at least fifty percent of the body boundary
is missing, we want to shift awareness and
perception to the space where the body is not.
We can call this "vastness" or "the void."

— Releasing our awareness into the vastness means
reaching and searching for any boundary or
border to the vastness.

— We want to also begin to discern what we are
experiencing. Is the vastness dark or bright in
visual or felt-sense appearance? What qualities
or functions of the vast Absolute are we discerning? When we are discerning qualities of the
Absolute, this is being done with the wisdom eye
coupled with our deep intuitive knowing.

— Can we perceive love, peace, Presence, stillness,
or something else?

— We then rest awareness and consciousness in this
nonverbal vastness. The meditative skill now is
to continuously surrender control, surrender our
personal effort, surrender getting anywhere.

Shikantaza Awakeness

The benefits of a regular, dedicated *shikantaza* practice are evident. Beginning with contacting the energy centers, the chakras, in our system, we are opening to the natural energy of the Absolute in our body. Each energy center in the body contains all the other energy centers. As we become deeply familiar with the chakras I teach in meditation, we open to the functioning of each center. For example, in Theravada Buddhist *samatha* practices, the wisdom eye, located in the center of the forehead, is indispensable.

The wisdom eye allows some of us to have inner sight in our meditation. For all of us wisdom eye affords us the ability to deepen and mature intuitive knowing. Intuitive knowing is knowing without reflection or comparison to any prior experiences.

We then orient to the unity of body and mind, which dissolves the conceptual separation between these two. We experience the unity of inner and outer energetic atmospheres. Finally, we open awareness into the vast void, the spaciousness Absence/emptiness of the Absolute.

I have witnessed in my students the grounding benefits of a regular and sustained *shikantaza* meditation practice. They gain greater comfort contacting and abiding in the Absolute. Whatever concerns or fears are activated by contact with the unending vastness of the unconditioned, they soften and fall away with sustained engagement. In other words, the students gain more comfort and ease abiding in and as the Absolute.

Many realize *shikantaza* Awakeness through my three-week Awakening retreat. I offer guided meditations deep into the Absolute, helping them to put down and drop all forms of identity while developing trust in the Absolute.

When they are open and able to fully surrender, the ripeness of *shikantaza* Awakeness can be experienced. This Awakeness is the expansion of awareness throughout the vastness of the Absolute. It can be realized as a deep unity or Oneness experience. It can additionally appear as the emptiness of all identity. It can then culminate in the deep knowing that the profound unity of love of the Absolute coupled with the shattering experience of Absence/emptiness is our true identity.

I often suggest my students begin formal *kōan* study after a first *kenshō* through *shikantaza* Awakeness.

KŌAN STUDY

ANOTHER ZEN AWAKENING path is formal *kōan* study. A *kōan* is a story, a spiritual riddle, a paradox of reality. Many *kōans* originated in live exchanges between deeply realized masters of Chan/Zen and dedicated students. It is difficult to communicate clearly the level and degree of intimacy that exists between a master and a committed student of many years. A slight change in expression or the use of an unusual word combination will spark the student in unimaginably beneficial ways and manners.

The sixth and seventh century in China was a robust time of Awakening in the Chan history. The teachers and masters were extremely sharp, with a honed edge to their Awakening that could instantly spark students into deep Awakening experiences. Witnesses recorded student-master exchanges in collections such as the *Mumonkan* (*The Gateless Gate*), the *Hekiganroku* (*Blue Cliff Record*), and others.

These *kōan* collections are used in my lineage and tradition. *Kōan* students work through these collections after passing the initial breakthrough *kōan*s we call the *dharmakaya kōan*s, which are the explosive *kōan*s of initial Awakening. For example, the three main *dharmakaya kōan*s I use with my students are "Mu," "Original Face," and "One Hand Clapping."

"Mu"

Introduction

"Mu" is Case 1 of the *Mumonkan* and, as such, is the quintessential *kōan*, the alpha and omega of realization. One can take up this *kōan* and continuously unfold and deepen realization endlessly. It is intended to cut off conceptual and rational thought, even words themselves. We must put everything down that we thought we knew, even our own identity, and surrender completely to be *mu*.

Mu is uncompromising. Words and flowery speech do not demonstrate understanding or resolution of *mu*. The roshi demands, "Do not tell me '*mu*.' Show me *mu*!"

My Translation

A monk resting in everyday mind asked Joshu, "Does that dog have Buddha nature?"

Master Joshu answered, "Mu."

(*Mu* means "no," "not," "without," or "no-thing.")

Mumon's Comment

To master Zen, you must pass the patriarch's barrier. To invite this subtle realization, you must completely cut off the allegiance to thoughts and preferences.

If this barrier is not passed, and the allegiance to thoughts and preferences is not cut off, then you will be like a hollow ghost resigned to the undergrowth.

Tell me now, what is the patriarch's barrier?

Why, it is this single word *mu*.

This is the portal of Zen.

Therefore, it is called the "Mumonkan of Zen."

If the patriarch's barrier is penetrated and passed, Master Joshu will appear face to face, while you walk hand in hand with the successive patriarchs, entangling your eyebrows with theirs, seeing with shared eyes and vision, hearing with shared ears.

Isn't that a delightful prospect?

Wouldn't you like to enter this very portal right here?

Arouse and direct your entire body with its three hundred and sixty bones and joints and its eighty-four thousand pores of the skin; summon up a spirit of Great Doubt and be one with *mu*.

Carry it close day and night with "don't know" mind.

It will be just as swallowing a red-hot iron ball, lodged deeply.

All the illusory ideas and delusive thoughts accumulated up to this moment will be vanquished, and in the fullness of time, inside and outside will be spontaneously perceived as ever united. You will know this truth on a cellular level.

A sudden explosive transformation will occur, and the heavens will be penetrated while the earth shakes in awe.

It will be as if the great sword of the valiant general Kan'u is nestled in your hand. When you meet the Buddha, kill him; when you meet the patriarchs, kill them.

On the precipice of life and death, perfect freedom is mandated; among the sixfold worlds and four modes of existence, there is frolicking in a merry and playful samadhi.

I say here and now, "How will you carry *mu?*"

Engage every ounce of intention and energy to work *mu*.

Hold on without breach—behold: A single spark, and the holy candle is lit!

Mugen's Comment

Carry it closely on the "tip of your breath" day and night
    without fail.
    Maintain "don't know" mind always.

Mumon's Verse

    An ordinary dog, the Buddha nature,

    The pronouncement, perfect and complete.

    Before you say it has or has not,

    You are a dead man on the spot.

Mugen's Verse

> No words come close
>
> To the impenetrable truth
>
> Abandon all hope
>
> Reveal true freedom

"Original Face"

Introduction

This is an interesting *kōan* to focus the student on the time-lessness of the Absolute without personal identity.

My Translation

Thinking of neither good nor evil,
What was your original face before your parents were born?

Mugen's Comment

We can see from this *kōan* that we clearly are not referring to our human face. What can an original face, before our parents were born, point to?

"One Hand Clapping"

Introduction

This *kōan* bridges the gap between the experiences of the Absolute in the prior two *kōan*s with the physical reality of everyday life. Can we find the Absolute in the mundane clapping of one hand?

My Translation

We have all heard and know the sound of two hands clapping. If one hand were put down and the remaining hand claps as before, what is that one-hand-clapping sound?

Mugen's Comment

Listen to the sound of no sound. Now show me your answer!

After one successfully completes these three *dharmakaya* *kōans* to the roshi's satisfaction, they begin the two hundred miscellaneous *kōans*. These are a loose compilation of small *kōans* to help invite a fuller Awakening, gently knocking down the stalactites and stalagmites of realization in a particular consciousness. Then one begins the hundreds of *kōans* in the *kōan* collections.

Kōan Path Awakeness

The initial Awakeness of the *kōan* path is *kenshō*. The resolution of each *kōan* in formal study results in a minor or major *kenshō* Awakeness experience. For example, nearly all students experience *kenshō* in the resolution of one or more of the *dharmakaya kōans*. This initial dropping away of mind and body opens the experience door. Each *kōan* that is resolved in us by the Absolute opens and expands the Awakeness a little more.

Kōans are quite direct and encourage us to surrender whatever we think we know and who we believe we are. This

Awakeness is related to the *shikantaza* Awakeness as it is an opening, a portal, to the Absolute. Yet the methodology is different.

Formal *kōan* study comprises roughly seven hundred *kōan*s if the full collection is passed. Interestingly, there are *kōan*s that teach us how to integrate Awakeness more deeply into our life. *Kōan*s also reveal how to speak and behave from the expanding Awakeness.

One of the fascinating benefits from *kōan* study is touching into so many teachers' realizations. I found inhabiting each being's consciousness in each *kōan* created an ability to shift and open in ways of which I was previously unaware. If a *kōan* had three participants, I would in turn enter into and inhabit each party's consciousness. It was then easier to feel into the ignorance, the ordinary not knowing, of the student inquiring of the master. Each teacher's and master's consciousness was riveting to abide within. Feeling and sensing the extent of depth of Awakeness was encouraging and normalizing to my developing Awakeness while working each *kōan*.

Working through the *kōan* collections while inhabiting the masters' consciousnesses expands our own consciousness to include their potential. In turn, their Awakeness becomes more active and strongly sensed or felt in the practitioner's consciousness and awareness. This leads us to the process of dharma transmission and the teaching and Awakening potency of the lineage.

DHARMA TRANSMISSION

STUDENTS WHO HAVE deeply practiced Zen and experienced the minor and major realizations of Awakeness can be invited to become dharma holders (assistant Zen teachers) at the discretion of their senior teacher. Late in our spiritual journey, we may also have an opportunity to engage and be guided through the advanced practices and spiritual training of dharma transmission with our teacher. Dharma transmission is necessary for a student to develop into a dharma teacher or sensei.

Mind-to-mind dharma transmission ensures that the Awakeness of the Absolute and profundity of Cessation are fully activated and functioning optimally. It is the direct transmission of Awakeness itself that is the subject of this process.

After many years of intimate one-on-one training with one's sensei (Zen teacher) or roshi (Zen master), dharma transmission concludes. The roshi observes the newly minted sensei to see how the Awakeness has landed and to what extent it is operationally active. Generally, the process concludes years later with a fine-tuning between student and teacher. At this time, the roshi is convinced by Awakeness itself that the student holds the identical view of the Awakeness of the Absolute and Cessation as the roshi, and these are operating as fully as possible.

Once this transmission of Awakeness is confirmed between new sensei and roshi, a final ceremony of Sealing the Mind-To-Mind Transmission is accomplished in the ceremony of Inka Shomei. Inka Shomei translates as "final seal of approval." This mind-to-mind seal is an undivided union of consciousness and awareness between teacher and student. It is a unity of mind that is unparalleled experientially. Not only do both teachers engage in deep practice, but there is a refinement, a purification, of practice. The roshi then names the student as a dharma heir and offers them the title of roshi, or Zen master. Zen master could be another name for Awakeness master or Absolute master.

When I was going through the process of dharma transmission with my teacher Mark Sando Mininberg, Roshi, I began to engage with teachers in other Zen traditions. I conversationally asked about their dharma transmission process. What I discovered is that each tradition has its own way of presenting this material and practices. Each lineage had similar processes but these were not identical.

I am a member of the White Plum Asanga. This is the body of transmitted teachers following in the Maezumi-

Roshi lineage. In my experience, transmission is a multiyear program of deeply advanced practices. We have a prescribed body of material we work in the dharma transmission process. It is not only completing all formal *kōan* study but also engaging with the advanced practices of the Five Ranks, Five Buddha Families, and hundreds of precepts *kōan*s, to name some of the practices. In the course of this fascinating process, the transmitting teacher and transmitting student share in an ongoing mind-to-mind transmission. This can culminate in Inka Shomei, the mind-to-mind seal mentioned above.

The effect of this multiyear intimate training is a perception of the lineage's Awakeness as a kind of energetic current running through and as the Absolute. At times when teaching I will feel the lineage current directing experiential teaching. There is a bodily felt wisdom that accompanies this current, this lineage flow. My task in these instances is to find the most precise words and language to communicate effectively both with language and energy.

As an active teacher, one of the benefits of this lineage current is its consistent feeding of my practice and teaching. Subtle areas of spiritual practice will be illuminated in the ripeness of time. The understanding I hold is constantly expanding and refining by maintaining an attunement to the lineage flow of the Absolute.

In the completion ceremony of transmission there remains a sense of how much more we need to practice, to learn. There is an authentic humility as an ongoing foundation to our spiritual journey. None of us will fully plumb the depths of the Absolute. The Absolute will always remain a profound mystery.

Lineage Awakeness

One of the influences of Confucianism on the Chan/Zen development is a deep reverence for history, for the lineage of past teachers and masters. The Awakeness of *kenshō* and Cessation is embodied in each Zen lineage. The Awakeness of all the roshis and senseis accumulates, embedded in the potent energy of the lineage.

As an entry point, a student can commit to a teacher and a lineage through the ceremony of *jukai*. In this ceremony, a student commits formally to an ongoing student-teacher relationship and receives the transmission of the Zen precepts. The precepts in the Chan/Zen tradition are held closely as wise guides on our unending journey of unfolding Awakening.

In the ceremony of *jukai*, the student also becomes a part of the direct energetic flow of the lineage stretching from Buddhism's founder, Shakyamuni Buddha, to the present day. *Jukai* transmits our spiritual roots from the source—the Absolute—through each generation of the matriarchs and patriarchs of our lineage to today's teachers.

The impact of *jukai* on the student is profound. To recognize and be welcomed into this important spiritual family is deeply, satisfyingly refreshing. It is a profound experience of belonging with the Absolute and all realized beings in the particular lineage. It's a welcoming ceremony that supports the student in coming home.

AWAKENESS FROM PERSONALITY

TO MORE FULLY UNDERSTAND the impact of Awakeness on personality, it's helpful to understand the effect of consciousness and changing consciousness on the journey of Awakeness.

Consciousness

An important part of pursuing a spiritual practice is developing, maturing, and Awakening consciousness. In maturing our consciousness, we are delving into our personal habitual way of perceiving, and we are learning how we execute the function of knowing following perception. We start this journey by understanding what contributes to the process of consciousness.

Consciousness can be recognized by its bearing, its felt sense of Beingness. When we make contact with consciousness and its aura, we know it. It feels as though there is something tangible here in awareness, something that is nonpersonal and objective.

Consciousness can also have a felt quality of timelessness. It does not feel constrained by the normal passage of time from future to present to past. We can experience consciousness as being "our consciousness," meaning a particular subjective perspective of experience can be present in consciousness. Yet consciousness is actually an undivided whole of the Absolute.

In the teachings of the Yogachara (which focuses on consciousness alone by delineating and engaging the levels of consciousness) and Zen schools of Buddhism, consciousness has eight particular discrete levels. In reality, consciousness has no levels. It is a unified Oneness of awareness, direct perception, and pure (nonconceptual) knowing. Yet for purposes of understanding the function and transformation of consciousness, it helps to separate consciousness into levels and investigate each one.

We will explore these eight levels starting with the first five consciousnesses and working our way up to the highest, the eighth consciousness, known as the storehouse consciousness or *alayavijnana*. I will present the experiential or felt-sense knowing of this eighth-level model of consciousness rather than the scholarly understanding.

First Five Levels of Consciousness

The first five levels of consciousness in Buddhism are the senses: sight, hearing, smell, taste, and touch. In effect, we receive raw data from the sense's contact with the inner and outer world.

This data can be received as welcome or unwelcome. For example, if you were tasting a food that was new to you, you might have neither a positive nor negative reaction, meaning you do not instantly like or dislike the new food's taste.

These first five levels of consciousness are only in operation when we are tracking sense data. If you are sitting with eyes closed in a quiet room, there would be little sense data available. Sense data is, therefore, conditioned and temporary. It is dependent upon an active stimulus for the senses to perceive or touch.

Sixth Level of Consciousness

The sixth level of consciousness is of thought and concept, where reactive perception is understood. Following the first five consciousnesses, which take in raw experiential data, the sixth consciousness processes the incoming data by applying memory, thought, and thought-concepts to identify the raw data and clarify its meaning and relationship to us as our customary self-identity. Really, this consciousness is informing us whether we like, dislike, or are neutral to the stimuli of the five senses. Our survival instincts need to evaluate all exterior and interior data to determine what is safe and what is dangerous.

The first six levels of consciousness are quite habitual. We have sensory contact with an object—say, an apple. We contact the apple with one or more of our senses. Then our thought and conceptual mind applies our history and experience to the object of an apple. This gives us a conclusion: "I like apples." Or perhaps apples are to be avoided because the last apple we ate was bad. The first six consciousnesses are straightforward and direct in function.

Seventh Level of Consciousness

The seventh level of consciousness is that of self-reflection, the ability to make mental inferences. We can draw conclusions about data or objects that we have not experienced before. If we see a new piece of fruit—a mango, for example—the seventh level of consciousness takes information about our direct experience with fruit similar to the mango and reaches an inferential conclusion about it.

The seventh level of consciousness is self-consciousness. In the seventh level of consciousness, we apply the incoming data to our experience, thoughts, and thought-concepts. We then compare this to our sense of self, our customary self-identity's previously established likes and dislikes. In part, this is where we conclude whether the new data or experience is favorable or unfavorable to us.

One contribution that the seventh level of consciousness makes to our overall sense of self is identifying with the results of our thoughts. When we reach a mental conclusion on any topic, we identify with that conclusion, meaning it attaches to our sense of self. We confirm this is our opinion and conclusion about that data object. Our ongoing conclusions about sense data constantly reaffirm the sense of me. Oh yes, I am someone who likes apples.

With deepening realization, we see that thoughts are often conditioned by the input we are receiving and our preferences for particular thought topics. We simply prefer some thought patterns over others. The ones we prefer or favor are part of the makeup of identity—of who we assert we are to ourselves and the world. In addition, realization of the Absolute deepens and changes our customary self-identity. Therefore, our likes and dislikes are also subject to alteration, modification, or outright change.

The seventh level of consciousness works in part by referencing the customary self-identity housed in the eighth level of consciousness—the *alayavijnana*.

Eighth Level of Consciousness, the *Alayavijnana*

The eighth level of consciousness, the *alayavijnana*, is often referred to as the storehouse consciousness. It is the source of the sense of self, that is, the ego or soul.

As sensory input enters into our perception, we take the raw data to the sixth level of consciousness to label it.

We then begin to create our desire or aversion to the new information in the seventh level of consciousness. Further, we apply our personal history of thought and concept to process the incoming data using our thoughts and concepts about it. In the seventh level, we are then also reflecting on whether the arising of the new data is something our sense of self desires, rejects, or is reticent about.

This processing of the first through seventh level of consciousness then creates a memory seed of experience. These memory seeds are called *bijas* in Buddhism.

Some *bijas* seem to be present at birth. This would help explain the Buddhist understanding of rebirth. Each lifetime has particular experiences, opinions, conceptual understandings, and beliefs. These experiences add *bijas* to the eighth level of consciousness, the *alayavijnana*. Some portion of the eighth level of consciousness transfers from lifetime to lifetime.

The conditioned *bijas* are significantly purified of meaning and history in the process of Awakening. In effect, some portion of the *bijas* are cleansed and purified back to their original pure nature of Absence. Absence is the primary felt-sense quality of the unmanifest workings of the Absolute in the Absolute realm. The inherent nature of clarity of the *bijas* makes them attracted to purity, and they seek cleansing through meditations, spiritual practices, and wholesome behavior (*sīla*).

Other *bijas* are added and subtracted with life experiences that are colored by judgments and opinions and by our sense

of self. These seeds accumulate in the storehouse consciousness. The eighth level is also the repository of our karma.
In effect, the collection of *bījas* influences our life direction.
This level of consciousness contains our life experiences, core
conceptual convictions, and karmic history bundled in one
location.

These *bījas* influence our thoughts, opinions, perspectives, desires, aversions, and overall attachments. The subjective perspective and conceptual opinion of the eighth
consciousness is what supports the belief in an ego: a conceptual conviction that I am a separate individual relying
upon my own actions to succeed in life. The cumulative
position of the *bījas* in the eighth consciousness leads us to
conclude we have a fixed opinion and perspective based upon
the orientation of the *bījas* to a particular topic or subject.
As we witness the *bījas* being purified and released through
realization of the Absolute by the Absolute, the individual
and collective *bījas* change, and with this change is a shift in
identity, karma, perspective, and opinion.

The spiritual seeker uses meditation and prayer to open
the eighth level of consciousness in part by gently questioning
and/or challenging the closely held sense of self. As our self is
modified or changed as a result of direct experience or realization, we are by default updating the storehouse consciousness. This then influences the seed collection in the eighth
level. We can purify or discard some seeds as our sense of self
is modified or changed through realization and Awakening.

Interestingly as we alter, purify, or release *bījas* from the *alayavijnana*, we are modifying and changing our karma and identity. Any time we alter or change our karma, we change and alter our perceived identity. Through direct realization of absolute truth, the Absolute, we change our karmic trajectory as well as who we take ourselves to be. This is the revolutionary aspect of maintaining an ongoing spiritual practice. We can change who we are as well as our karmic stream's direction.

The eighth consciousness seems to also include the potency of realization—that is, our Buddha nature or true nature. Embedded in our storehouse consciousness are all levels, types, and kinds of realization up to full Buddhahood—that is, being fully and thoroughly awake or realized. This is true because consciousness is an undivided wholeness of the manifest functioning of the Absolute. The eighth level of consciousness is already completely pure and realized. We need to work through and appropriately question our assumptions and core conceptual convictions to clear away what is false and conditioned, replacing it with what is always pure and unconditioned.

Awakeness's Impact on Personality

One of the major touchstones of a deep Awakening, whether a Zen *kenshō* experience or a Theravada Cessation experience, is the impact on personality. An Awakening experience is considered deep when it dramatically impacts the personality.

In the traditional Theravada Buddhist understanding of Awakening, the first level is called "stream entry." This means that one's consciousness enters the stream of Awakeness and merges with it. This entry into the stream of Awakening is confirmed by a major shift in the person's view of and from their personality. The personality is not gone, but the personality is no longer the primary vantage point.

This awake consciousness now views itself and the world from a more inclusive, wholesome perspective. The viewpoint shifts from seeing the personality as the foundation to seeing the true nature as the foundation. "True nature" is the term used to mean the qualities and functions of the Absolute in one particular consciousness. If an awake person were asked who they were, they would respond with either "I do not know" or, from the unity-love function of the Absolute, "Everything is a Oneness."

Consciousness and True Nature

Our storehouse, or eighth level of consciousness, contains the seeds of full realization. From the Absolute truth abiding in the Absolute realm, we can experience pure emptiness, pure awareness, pure Presence, and pure love. Pure awareness is direct awareness without conceptual reference. This means we can perceive data without comparing it to our concepts, thoughts, or life experience. The incoming data bypasses our thought consciousness (sixth level of consciousness) and self-consciousness (seventh level) and arrives directly at the storehouse consciousness (eighth level).

In addition, the *alayavijnana* also contains our intuitive understandings. This is the location of the wisdom received through the dharma eye. When we perceive some inner or outer information, we can meet that new perception with the intuitive consciousness of the *alayavijnana*. Again, this avoids the application of our thoughts and concepts as well as our seeking to determine how it applies, or impacts, our sense of self.

Changes to Consciousness After Awakening

As Awakeness is experienced and resides actively in our consciousness, our consciousness changes. In the following section, I offer some understanding and explanation of how Awakeness impacts and influences the upper levels of our consciousness. We start with the eighth level as the store-house, the repository. When the eighth level changes, the whole downstream flow is significantly altered and changed.

Changes to the Eighth Level of Consciousness

With *kenshō*, the Absolute is seen, witnessed, in the *alaya-vijnana*. The purity of the Absence core quality of the *bījas* is witnessed to a penetrating depth. The prior *bījas* that were flavored by a belief in a core wound—such as "I am bad," "I am unlovable," "I am worthless"—release the quality of self-identity and become transparent. This is another way in which the brightness of the manifest function of the Absolute shines in our particular consciousness.

Our consciousness is the undivided whole of all of consciousness. The "I" becomes a *tathāgatagarba* (seed of Buddhahood or Buddha nature) after *satori* or a significant experience of Cessation and is significantly converted after a *Daigo-tettei* Awakening.

Awakeness can also result in an experience of Cessation, as discussed above. Should the experience of Cessation be a sustained experience, typically thirty minutes or more, it can flower into the fruit of *Nibbāna*. *Nibbāna* is the ceasing, the Cessation, of all mentality and materiality. In the experience of *Nibbāna* the *bījas*, the seeds, of the *alayavijnana* are converted from self-identity *bījas* to Absolute or Absence *bījas*. In *Nibbāna*, the eighth level of consciousness converts from a storehouse of personal memories and imprints of self-behavior to Absence as the predominant felt sense of identity.

After a *Daigo-tettei* Awakening, the eighth consciousness becomes perceived as an undivided whole with the Absolute, alternating in the interplay of the manifest and unmanifest functions of the Absolute.

Changes to the Seventh Level of Consciousness

Before an Awakening experience, we see our concepts, our thought definitions, of reality as sacred and singularly authentic. In our view, these concepts are real and, like the forces of gravity, cannot be challenged or questioned.

In the experience of any spiritual realization, particularly an Awakening experience, concepts, along with the customary sense of self, are dropped. Zen Master Dōgen famously applied the phrase "falling away of mind and body" as a shorthand description of Awakening.

We can therefore see that the concepts the seventh level of consciousness generates fade as we move into the direct experience of pure awareness. This is the experiential territory of no concept and no thought. It is knowing through direct contact. What is water? Take a sip, then you will know with the certainty of direct experience what is real, what is water.

After a *satori*-level Awakening, true nature shifts to become the foundation of identity. Concepts are then useful to explain ideas but have no greater value than a calculator resting on your desk. When you need to add a string of numbers, it is essential. Once that task is complete, you turn off the calculator and replace it on your desk until it is needed for its specific function.

Changes to the Sixth Level of Consciousness

The raw data received by each of our five senses (sight, hearing, smell, touch, and taste) is compared to our history and memory to find a close similar experience. When we find that data, we apply the concept associated with that prior memory to the current direct experience. Predictably, this colors the present moment experience by confining it to the relationship with the prior memory. This limits and reduces the impact and subtleness of whatever we are in direct experience with in this moment.

With increasingly sustained experiences of resting in our inner spaciousness, we learn to relax, to open, without expectation of reliance on prior memories or thought to interfere with our direct knowing.

In Awakening, we directly experience the Absolute and its associated qualities of Absence or Presence. This is an unmediated, direct knowing experience that cannot be compared to anything in our past. Just this! Right here! This is what we know.

Our reliance on thoughts for identification of our outer and inner world can lessen and fall away. Thoughts can begin to be a useful tool when needed—and only when needed. Otherwise, we can rest directly in the felt sense of our experience, in the experiential truth of this moment.

Deconstruction of Personality Beliefs

As infants mature, they develop language skills from their family and early caregivers. Along with these early language skills comes social information. This social information includes what we take as facts, such as gravity, time, past/

present/future, and other foundational understandings of how our world works.

The truthfulness and accuracy of these beliefs and convictions from our early life is unquestioned. We simply do not challenge the underlying assumptions we hold from our family about how the world works and, more importantly, who we are in this vast world.

The most deeply held convictions and beliefs interplay with our identity, self-image, and our social or relational connectivity. Our self-identity is an amalgamation of mirroring and feedback we received in our early life. If our early caregivers praised us for being happy, for example, we might include "happy" as a component of our self-identity. How we did in school would also be a characterizing self-definition. These various definitions are then held and arranged in a specific order to arrive at our inner sense of me.

Should a new acquaintance reflect our inner sense of me in a manner that feels accurate, we feel they are not only quite bright but, more importantly, also get us. We generally like these people.

Conversely, if someone does not mirror or reflect who we are in conformity with our self-perception, we feel they are not perceptive and do not get us. We tend to dislike these people.

In ongoing spiritual practice, particularly the gradual purification-of-mind Theravada Buddhist practices or the direct Awakeness Chan/Zen path, we meet and test the various assumptions about ourselves that we hold dear. We orient toward truth and authenticity. Whenever a particular identity is highlighted through life events, we examine that identity and its history to determine if it is accurate today. If we conclude it is not accurate, we must be willing to update it, discard it, or simply put it down. If, conversely, we find it is thoroughly accurate, we hold it close as a confirmed truth today. In years to come and through deeper spiritual contact with the Absolute, though, this truth may later be revealed as no longer accurate. It is a never-ending process.

Working with Preverbal Memories

Most people fail to realize that they are operating, in part, from preverbal beliefs, understandings, and convictions. We need to know how to identify and work with these ancient memories. To understand how the preverbal memories function, it's helpful to understand how they are set or structured in our psyche.

We are each born lacking any verbal language skills. In addition, we are each born in a unity with the Presence and love of the Absolute. We arrive into this world and life in a Oneness, a unity. We presume everyone else is in the same experience of unity.

The body boundary is one of the earliest preverbal self-identities. In time, the infant begins to realize that hunger and other infant needs are entirely contained in this bodily structure. The infant concludes that the inside of this body from the skin, the body boundary, is "me." Whatever is outside the body boundary is "not me."

This idea of the self and other conclusions reached because of this developing me erode the unity, the merged nonduality, with the Presence of the Absolute. The nonverbal infant will also have other experiences that land as unquestionable primary truths. Because these experiences are established before learning language, they are not stored in memory in verbal form.

In spiritual practice, we need to be open to observing these nonverbal beliefs and convictions. Identifying preverbal beliefs begins with tracking our behaviors and attitudes. Nonverbal convictions and beliefs generally present as situations when we feel extremely stubborn about an issue that seems trivial. We feel overinvested in a particular topic or issue. It defies our logic to be so fixated on an issue that we view as trivial.

Preverbal issues typically need to be worked on with a teacher. It is very difficult to see the preverbal issue and be with it without using words or concepts.

As we work these various seen and unseen issues in our personality and sense of self, we are concurrently opening to integrate and embody our deepening understanding of reality. This is the part of the path I call living Awakeness.

CONCLUSION

Awakening is becoming more prevalent in our world.

BEING AWARE and intentional with the qualities or functions of Awakeness in these various spiritual practices deepens our experiential knowing.

As we cultivate these qualities and functions, we align more closely with the alive Awakeness of the Absolute. This lets us embody and express these qualities more clearly and reliably.

We have seen how these practices and meditations impact our sense of self, our belief in the permanence of temporal reality, and our dissatisfaction with aspects of our daily life. We can see more deeply into these areas and the corresponding issues to more closely align to truth and to express our knowing understanding as an authenticity grounded in the reality of the Absolute.

Awakening is becoming more prevalent in our world and in this particular time in history. There is an inner ripeness that is manifesting in the world as an increasing intimacy with the Absolute. The process and support for Awakening has never been more accessible as in modern times. What is missing is an understanding of what happens in Awakening and what we do thereafter to embody and sustain the Awakening.

In this book, we have seen a number of the qualities that manifest and appear following the flowering of Awakening in a particular consciousness. These qualities define the depth and quality of integration that is occurring. Intentionally identifying with and learning to employ these qualities of our true nature supports the deepening of Awakening and the integration of the unconditioned qualities of the Absolute Awakening in our particular consciousness. Through sustained work with these qualities, we further their rooted existence and learn to depend on their functioning as we move through our daily life.

I encourage you to invest time slowly integrating each quality of Awakeness in your life and spiritual practice. Deeply examine each quality of Awakeness, taking the time to investigate your history and beliefs associated with it. Let yourself slowly open to reveal any limiting opinions about these qualities. Be willing to experience each quality anew on a nonconceptual level.

By learning how the self or personality structuring affects our experience of these qualities, we reveal what has been hidden in the dark recesses of our consciousness and identity. We enliven and invite the brilliant brightness of the manifest Absolute, particularly the love, nonduality, and Presence of the Absolute. As we engage these important qualities more neutrally, we are changed.

Know that this is a lifelong process—perhaps even multiple lifetimes. We can only work with qualities that are apparent, within reach, or in view. Take up these qualities with gentleness and respect. Allow your ripeness to develop at its own speed; it can never be forced. Know that some of our personality beliefs and convictions will be in opposition to the truth we are experiencing and beginning to live. Invite inner change.

Enjoy the majesty and wonder of this incredible journey.

AFTERWORD

*I did not know how to pick this question up or
put it down.*

MY FIRST BIG Awakening, or *satori*, experience was brought about by a line in a book. I was reading a Buddhist text with a reference to the *Diamond Sutra* that said "produce the thought that is nowhere supported." That instruction instantly perplexed and confounded me. I could almost hear the gears of my mind grinding to a shuddering halt. I did not know how to pick this question up or put it down. It was wedged in my psyche.

To address this mystery, I decided to explore the levels of consciousness. Revealing thoughts arise based upon sensory input. I started with my eyes open, perceiving through sight. I then traced the raw visual data from the front of my eye, through the eye structure, optic nerve, and into the brain.

When I reached the source of sight, which was deep in my brain, I placed a mental marker.

I then took up the hearing sense. I heard something outside my body. I followed the movement of raw sounds from sense data to interpretation and the judgment of relationship to see if I liked, disliked, or was neutral to the sound. As with the sight exercise, I traced the workings of hearing from outside through the mechanics of the ear and arrived at a spot in my brain where sound became known. As before, I left a mental marker at the source of sound. I proceeded with the senses of taste, touch, and feel to trace them from external data to the point of fully knowing the data based on my thoughts, concepts, history, memory, and sense of self.

When I had traced all the senses back to the source of meaning within my brain, an inner explosion occurred. All ways of knowing mind and body vanished. There was no I. Every way I recognized me to myself—such as my body, my thoughts, my memories, my emotions—was absent, completely out of range. I saw and was pure Absence, pure love, pure Presence, pure awareness (direct knowing) at once.

Within this beautiful weave of the Absolute, I saw this was me. This was who I really and truly was. I finally felt I had resolved all doubts; all insecurities were vanquished in this absence of self. The unacknowledged parts of me that I carried with deep shame were freed by the unconditioned love of the Absolute. I was not my worst life behavior. I was not my karma.

The overwhelming waves of love revealed that this, the Absolute, was my true nature. Within the waves of pure love and pure Presence, I could also sense qualities of true nature, my true nature, our true nature, no one's true nature.

———

ACKNOWLEDGMENTS

I OFFER MY deepest gratitude and thanks to the two lineages that have been so deeply important to me in my practice and now my teaching. My teaching originates in and is an expression of the energetic flow of wisdom from each lineage as it is deeply experienced and presented by its teachers throughout space and time.

I am also grateful to my students, particularly those training as teachers. Their wholesome desire to experience and express these profound practices is deeply heartwarming to me.

Thank you to the team that brought this book to fruition—Alex Hennig, Carra Simpson, Lynn Slobogian, Eva van Emden, and Jazmin Welch.

GLOSSARY

Absence: A synonym for "emptiness" in Buddhism. It is a quality of reality where there is nothing apparent to ordinary perception, yet something substantial and significant is present and perceived intuitively, directly through experiential contact.

absence of self: The experience of the customary self-identity being increasingly transparent and difficult to locate within. Also known as no-self.

Absolute: The source of all life animation and manifestation of all form and formless reality.

Absolute realm: The realm where the Absolute can be directly and deeply perceived, experienced, and merged with. The Absolute can function as unmanifest or manifest. The unmanifest is characterized by dark blackness, Absence (emptiness), deep peace, and profound stillness. The manifest, on the other hand, appears as a brilliant brightness of purity, pure, unconditioned love, pure Presence (Beingness) and pure awareness (awareness without historical references).

ānāpānasati: See breath awareness meditation.

authentic: A description of something that originates directly in the unconditioned Absolute.

Awakening and **First Awakening:** The Absolute Awakening to itself from the dream of solely being a separate me. Awakening is an experience in which the sense of self becomes transparent to our self-perception, we are deeply experiencing the undivided nondual love of the Absolute, and we have the aha moment of recognizing that no-self and unity are our true identity. First Awakening is an experience that contains (1) a deep experience of absence of self, (2) clear seeing of one's true nature as one's true identity, and (3) a thorough unity experience where all is one, or everything is a fabric of Oneness.

awareness: Perception, with or without consciousness, of internal and external events unfolding.

Beingness: Unconditioned Presence.

brahmavihāras: Ancient Buddhist heart meditations that open our awareness to unconditioned qualities of our true nature such as equanimity (*upekkhā*), empathetic joy (*muditā*), compassion (*karunā*), unconditioned love (*mettā*), and innate goodness, to name a few.

breath awareness meditation: Called *ānāpānasati* from the Pali *ānāpāna* (breath) and *sati* (awareness). Typically, the first meditation given to new Theravada Buddhist students by the Buddha. This practice concentrates and purifies the mind through turning away from the habituated thinking and routine concepts. This practice can lead to the deepest level of meditative concentration called *jhāna*. (Please see my book *Practicing the Jhānas* for details on this practice.)

Cessation: The experience of complete merging into the pristine stillness and the unmeasurable depth of peace and the rich Absence (emptiness) of the unmanifest Absolute, in which all mentality and materiality cease. Another name for a potential enlightenment experience, as there will be experiential changes following Cessation that permanently change the self-identity. Also known as *nirodha.*

Chan: The Chinese Buddhist tradition of using *kōans* and *shikantaza* (silent illumination meditation) to open and directly experience Cessation and likely a *kenshō*, an Awakening experience.

concentration meditation: A collection of meditations in which the meditator stays with one meditative object, prioritizing it over all other sense data or experience.

conceptual knowing and **nonconceptual knowing**: Conceptual knowing is when we compare a present experience with our memories of prior life experiences. Nonconceptual knowing is direct knowing without comparing the present direct memory with our history.

consciousness: Awareness coupled with ordinary and intuitive knowing.

core wound: The inner experience of instability or the perception of weakness often found in the solar plexus area of our body. Also known in psychological terms as core ego deficiency.

Daigo-tettei: The third level of Awakening experience (*kensho*) in the Zen tradition, in which the self-identity drops away and is not reactivated.

defilements: The Buddhist defilements are (1) desire or greed, (2) aversion or ill will, and (3) delusion. It is understood that while everyone has all three of these defilements, we each have an inherent proclivity for being predominantly a desire or an aversion type.

dharma: Teaching or universal law. Also known as *dhamma*.

dual unity: A state where the infant is in an undifferentiated state of individuation and is thus in a nondual union with all other beings until the self-identity lands in the individual consciousness.

dukkha: The first noble truth of Buddhism that human life contains unsatisfactoriness or suffering.

felt sense: Intuitive perception of what is not visually apparent.

first arrow and **second arrow**: Concepts the Buddha used in his teaching. The first arrow is pain or initial discomfort. The second arrow is the commentary, story, or resistance to the first arrow.

First Awakening: See Awakening.

generativeness: The manner in which the Absolute learns and developmentally expands. Because the Absolute contains all unconditioned reality, and everything in the Absolute is here and now, it was challenging for me to find suitable language to express how the Absolute develops. The Absolute depends on the conditioned to realize the unconditioned. As we each experience Awakening in our consciousness, we are further informing the Absolute, and this new information is assimilated. The term "generative" was the best I could find to describe this process of symbiosis between the conditioned and unconditioned.

hara: Area in the belly about two fingerwidths below the navel and about two to three fingerwidths beneath the surface of the skin. It is an energy center, called a chakra in the yogic tradition. It is an important inner seat of the Absolute that is primarily nonconceptual.

innate goodness: The inherent quality of our true nature; goodness not dependent on any manner of doing or way of being.

jhāna: The third level of concentration, also called absorption concentration; a nondual state with complete awareness, no thoughts, and no discernible self.

jhāna **factors**: Available in all meditations, these are (1) applied awareness (*vitakka*), (2) sustained awareness (*vicāra*), (3) joy (*pīti*), (4) bliss (*sukha*), and (5) one-pointedness (*ekaggatā*).

karma: A complex compilation of all past experiences into present-moment reality. In other words, whatever we have done in the past conditions our perception of this moment. Engaging actively with meditation or spiritual practices helps dissolve past karma.

karunā: Compassion, a kindhearted holding that allows us, and others, to be with our pain and to persevere. An unconditioned quality of our true nature.

kasina: A mind-made, disklike object that can be perceived meditatively by either visual or felt-sense contact. There are color *kasinas*, four element *kasinas* (earth, water, fire, and air), and two very subtle *kasinas*, light *kasina* and space *kasina*.

kenshō: Seeing into one's true nature; from the Zen tradition's map of Awakening.

kōan: A spiritual paradox that cannot be resolved by the thinking mind; spiritual intuition and realization offer the perfect solution.

levels of concentration: (1) Momentary concentration, (2) access concentration, and (3) absorption concentration (*jhāna*).

mettā: Usually translated as "loving-kindness," it is the unconditioned love of the Absolute.

muditā: Empathetic joy, or the joy we feel at another's success, happiness, or joy. Their joy or success feels indistinguishable from our joy or success. An unconditioned quality of our true nature.

Nibbāna: An experience of Cessation in which all materiality and mentality cease. Also known as *nirvāna*.

nondual state: A perception in which one's consciousness is experienced as an undivided unity with all of life, a completeness with no remainders or exclusions.

no-self: An experience in which the customary self-identity is absent (or transparent) and a unity experience of all is one is concurrently present.

off-the-cushion meditation and **on-the-cushion meditation**: Reference to the importance of continuity. For a meditation to reach its furthest depths of experience, we need to maintain ongoing contact when seated in formal meditation as well as while navigating our life.

Oneness: The function of the Absolute and all universes is a unified, indivisible unity.

particular realm (formless *jhāna*): The world can be viewed as being composed of form (tangible structure) and formless (no discernible structure). In the deep concentration of breath awareness meditation, we can merge into profound qualities of the Absolute, such as boundless space, boundless consciousness, boundless nothingness, and neither perception nor non-perception. The experience of merging with these qualities is known as entering the particular realm.

Presence: Experiential contact with the Beingness quality of this present moment.

resistances: Psychological or emotional patterns of mind or behavior that restrict awareness from contacting qualities of our true nature, including a First Awakening.

samadhi: Very deep concentration meditation. Samadhi would be referring to either access concentration or absorption concentration (*jhāna*).

samatha: Another term for the purification-of-mind practices in Theravada Buddhism that teach the student to focus on one meditative object at a time, to unify awareness while balancing energy and meditative concentration. *Samatha* translates as concentration, serenity, or tranquility.

satori: The sustained *kenshō* experience of seeing into one's true nature. In *satori*, the experience is both more far-reaching and more sustaining than in *kenshō*. *Satori* will awaken in 51 percent or more of an individual consciousness for a shift in identity from the customary personality view to true nature.

self-identity: The psychological patterns of mind and behavior that define who we are to ourselves; self-concept; self-recognition.

shikantaza: The Japanese name for silent illumination meditation.

silent illumination meditation: The Chinese Chan Buddhist meditation of bringing awareness to unify (1) body/mind, (2) inside/outside, and (3) vastness without conceptual boundaries.

source: The Absolute, the source of all creation and manifestation. Cessation is the origin of the Absolute.

suchness: A term for the Zen expression of true reality, "not two, not one"; the realization that duality is a position of mind. It is resting in and abiding with the Absolute without separation or division. Also called thusness.

sutras: The Sanskrit term for sermons or religious talks offered by Shakyamuni Buddha; known as *suttas* in Pali.

Theravada Buddhism: The tradition of Buddhism maintaining the traditional meditative practices of the Buddha.

thought-concept: The concepts and ideas we construct, and the mentalizing we perform, in an attempt to define and control our inner and outer world.

three pure precepts: Guides for our lives as committed practitioners. (1) Cease from evil—stop taking intentional selfish action that will harm others. (2) Do only good—take action that is consistent with the love, Presence, and Absence of the Absolute. (3) Do good for others—take action that will benefit as many beings as possible, including ourselves.

true nature: The true, core foundation of unconditioned reality. This refers to qualities of the Absolute embedded in our particular consciousness.

upekkhā: Equanimity, a feeling of perfect balance. Everything that is occurring inside or outside of us is exactly right in this moment. An unconditioned quality of our true nature.

wisdom eye: The functioning of inner seeing or deep intuitive knowing associated with the chakra in the center of the forehead. In the Zen tradition, this is referred to as the dharma eye.

Zen Buddhism: The Buddhist tradition evolving from Chinese Chan Buddhism, in which Awakening is the primary objective.

ABOUT THE AUTHOR

Stephen Mugen Snyder, Roshi, began practicing daily meditation in 1976. Since then, he has studied Buddhism extensively—investigating and engaging in Zen, Tibetan, Theravada, and Western nondual traditions. He was authorized to teach in the Theravada Buddhist tradition in 2007 and in the  Zen Buddhist schools of Sōtō and Rinzai in 2022. Stephen is a senior student of Mark Sando Mininberg, Roshi, and a transmitted teacher in the White Plum Asanga—the body of teachers in the Maezumi-Roshi lineage.

Stephen's resonant and warmhearted teaching style engages students around the globe through in-person and online retreats, as well as one-on-one coaching. He encourages students to turn toward their true nature and, with realization of their true nature, embody their true identity. Stephen is the author of five books, including *Liberating the Self, Trust in Awakening, Demystifying Awakening,* and *Buddha's Heart.* He coauthored *Practicing the Jhānas.* For more information, please visit awakeningdharma.org.

DID YOU BENEFIT FROM *LIVING AWAKENESS?*

SHARE YOUR PRAISE

Did this book offer new insights into Buddhist teachings that are benefiting your daily life or interactions? If so, a review shared through your favorite online retailer would be warmly welcomed. A few minutes of your time could help others find this book and benefit as you have.

PLACE A BULK ORDER

Would you like to share this book with a group or a class? Please be in touch! We can offer bulk discounts for orders of ten or more copies to most locations. Please write to hello@ awakeningdharma.org.

KEEP IN TOUCH

For more about Stephen's books, workshops, and other offerings, please visit awakeningdharma.org.

Demystifying Awakening: A Buddhist Path of Realization, Embodiment, and Freedom
HARDCOVER • 978-1-7347810-6-9 • $24.95
PAPERBACK • 978-1-7347810-4-5 • $16.95
E-BOOK • 978-1-7347810-5-2 • $9.95
PUBLISHED MARCH 2022

A practice path in the process of Awakening—in this lifetime. *Demystifying Awakening* clearly explains experiences of Awakening, highlighting the natural resistances and how to work with them; outlines steps for developing a wholesome livelihood: the natural embodiment of realization; and offers extensive meditations and practices that support each step on the path.

Buddha's Heart: Meditation Practice for Developing Well-Being, Love, and Empathy
PAPERBACK • 978-1-7347810-2-1 • $16.95
E-BOOK • 978-1-7347810-3-8 • $9.95
PUBLISHED NOVEMBER 2020

An original and clear path to the powerful *brahmavihāras*—ancient Buddhist heart practices. These practices offer rich, soothing support for the soul and a portal to spiritual awakening and deepening self-realization. *Buddha's Heart* teaches what seems counterintuitive but is undeniably true: the more we open our hearts, the more resilient and flexible we are. And the more authentically vulnerable we are, the safer and more protected we become.

Stress Reduction for Lawyers, Law Students, and Legal Professionals: Learning to Relax

PAPERBACK • 978-1-7347810-0-7 • $14.95

E-BOOK • 978-1-7347810-1-4 • $9.95

PUBLISHED SEPTEMBER 2020

A practical guide for a more relaxed and enjoyable legal career—authored by a retired lawyer and senior meditation teacher. This book offers straightforward techniques to identify the events that cause stress in your work, apply practices that support deep relaxation, and develop greater satisfaction in your work and personal life.

Practicing the Jhānas: Traditional Concentration Meditation as Presented by the Venerable Pa Auk Sayadaw

PAPERBACK • 978-1-59030-733-5 • $22.95

E-BOOK • 978-0-8348-2282-5 • $17.99

PUBLISHED DECEMBER 2009

COAUTHORED WITH TINA RASMUSSEN

A clear and in-depth presentation of the traditional Theravada concentration meditation known as *jhāna* practice, developed from practicing *jhāna* meditation in retreat under the guidance of one of the great living meditation masters, the Venerable Pa Auk Sayadaw.